BUYING TRAVEL SERVICES ON THE INTERNET

Related Books from CommerceNet

Buying a Home on the Internet by Robert Irwin
Buying a Car on the Internet by Jeremy Lieb

CommerceNet is a nonprofit industry association for companies promoting and building electronic commerce solutions on the Internet. Launched in April 1994 in Silicon Valley, CA, its membership has grown to more than 500 companies and organizations worldwide. They include the leading banks, telecommunications companies, VANs, ISPs, on-line services, software and service companies, as well as end-users, who together are transforming the Internet into a global electronic marketplace. For membership information, please contact CommerceNet at telephone: (408) 446-1260, extension 214; fax: (408) 446-1268; URL: htp://www.commerce.net. For information regarding CommerceNet Press, contact Loël McPhee at loel@commerce.net.

BUYING TRAVEL SERVICES ON THE INTERNET

DURANT IMBODEN

CommerceNet Press

McGraw-Hill
New York   San Francisco   Washington, D.C.   Auckland   Bogotá
Caracas   Lisbon   London   Madrid   Mexico City   Milan
Montreal   New Delhi   San Juan   Singapore
Sydney   Tokyo   Toronto

Library of Congress Cataloging-in-Publication Data
Applied for.

McGraw-Hill

A Division of The McGraw·Hill Companies

Copyright © 1999 by Durant Imboden. All rights reserved. Printed in the United States of America. Except as permitted under the United States Copyright Act of 1976, no part of this publication may be reproduced or distributed in any form or by any means, or stored in a data base or retrieval system, without the prior written permission of the publisher.

1 2 3 4 5 6 7 8 9 0   DOC/DOC   9 0 9 8 7 6 5 4 3 2 1 0 9

ISBN 0-07-134871-9

The sponsoring editor for this book was Susan Barry, the editing supervisor was Tom Laughman, the editing liaison was Patricia V. Amoroso, and the production supervisor was Elizabeth J. Strange. It was set in Times Roman by North Market Street Graphics.

Printed and bound by R. R. Donnelley & Sons Company.

This publication is designed to provide accurate and authoritative information in regard to the subject matter covered. It is sold with the understanding that neither the author nor the publisher is engaged in rendering legal, accounting, or other professional service. If legal advice or other expert assistance is required, the services of a competent professional person should be sought.

> *—From a declaration of principles jointly adopted by a committee of the American Bar Association and a committee of publishers.*

 This book is printed on recycled, acid-free paper containing a minimum of 50% recycled de-inked fiber.

To Cheryl, my travel companion since we crossed the Pacific together on the USNS *General Hugh N. Gaffey* in 1963, and to our fellow travelers: Cedar, Thatcher, Anders, Holly, and Pippa.

C O N T E N T S

ACKNOWLEDGMENTS

Writing may be a lonely occupation, but authors depend on other people for success. This book wouldn't have been possible without:

Loel McPhee at www.commerce.net, who came up with the idea.

Jaclyn Easton at www.strikingitrich.com, who was drafted into helping Loel find a writer with a knowledge of travel and the Internet.

Mandy Hass at about.com, who pitched me to Jaclyn Easton without my knowledge (and lined up an appearance on Jaclyn's *Log On USA* radio program in the bargain).

Susan Barry at www.mcgraw-hill.com, who bought the book and has been a wonderfully responsive and supportive editor.

Lew Grimes, my agent at www.bookagency.com, who ably negotiated the contract with McGraw-Hill.

Yedida Soloff at www.mcgraw-hill.com, who kept me in the loop during the book's editorial and production process.

Tom Laughman, my copy editor at North Market Street Graphics in Lancaster, Pennsylvania, who saved me from the consequences of my inconsistencies and errors.

And last but not least:

My parents, *George and Lois Imboden,* for introducing me to travel at an early age; and . . .

The *U.S. Navy,* for supplying transportation until I was old enough to cross oceans at my own expense.

BUYING TRAVEL SERVICES ON THE INTERNET

1

CHAPTER

INTRODUCTION

The Internet is an on-line cornucopia of travel information. Unfortunately, its millions of Web pages are scattered randomly across thousands of computers in 100 or more countries. It's easy to see why the Internet has been described as "the Library of Congress without a catalog."

Finding useful travel sites on the Web can be a hit-or-miss effort with the leading on-line directories and search engines. Search on the phrase "Venice restaurant," and you're likely to find a Denny's in Los Angeles when you're really looking for a *trattoria* in Italy. To save time and frustration, you need a convenient starting point for your on-line explorations—and that's the role this book is designed to play.

Because I've done the legwork for you, *Buying Travel Services on the Internet* can cut your Web search time by 75 percent or more, but that's just the beginning. This book will also help you find *high-quality information* that you might miss if you were surfing without a guide. So, prop this book against your computer monitor, reach for your mouse, and start planning your next vacation or business trip on-line.

HOW TO USE THIS BOOK

Buying Travel Services on the Internet is organized into five major topics:

1. **Getting started:** On-line travel agencies, guidebook publishers, maps, passports and visas, packing tips, health information, and worldwide weather forecasts
2. **Getting around:** Traveling by air, rail, bus, road, and water at home and abroad
3. **Getting settled:** Accommodations, ranging from five-star hotels to campgrounds where the only stars are overhead
4. **Special-interest travel:** Web sites devoted to theme parks, accessible travel, family trips, gay/lesbian vacations, and active/adventure travel
5. **Destinations:** A guide to the leading sources of travel information for North and South America, Europe, Africa and the Middle East, Asia, and the South Pacific

In each section of the book, you'll find scores of Web addresses (URLs) that I've picked as the best sources of information on the featured subtopics. In the first four sections, I've also included hefty doses of general advice and travel tips.

As you plan your trip, simply use the table of contents or the index to locate the subtopic that interests you—for example, *packing* or *Switzerland*. Then, go to the appropriate pages, read the background information, and pick the sites you'd like to visit on the Web.

To access a Web site, you'll need to type its URL (Web shorthand for "Uniform Resource Locator") in the "address" blank at the top of your Web browser's window. Here's an example:

http://goeurope.miningco.com

In many newer browsers, you don't even need to type the prefix. Just type goeurope.miningco.com, and your browser (Internet Explorer, Netscape Navigator, or Opera) will whisk you off to the Web site.

A few caveats:

- Some pages can take a long time to display on your monitor. Such sluggishness may be caused by a slow Web server, Internet congestion, too many hops (or connection points) between your location and the server, or a page that's heavy on photos, artwork, and other graphics. Be patient, and the page should finish downloading before too long.

- Web sites sometimes change their home addresses, switch the URLs of individual pages, or go out of business without warning. The "little guys" aren't the only offenders—I've seen major sites like Microsoft Expedia, Sabena Airlines, and the Paris Tourist Office change URLs with annoying frequency.

- When your browser can't find a Web page, it will display an error message. The sidebar shows the most common error messages and what to do about them.

COMMON ERROR MESSAGES, *CONT.*

To help you cope with the unpredictable nature of Web-masters and their Web sites, I'm offering a "freshness guarantee":

For as long as this edition of Buying Travel Services on the Internet *continues to have significant sales, I'll post updates for changed or broken URLs on a special Web page.*

These URL updates are organized by chapter, in the same sequence as the listings in this book, so it won't take you long to find them. The Web site's URL is:

http://www.writing.org/travel.htm

Also, if you encounter a broken link and don't find a correction or acknowledgment on the update page, feel free to e-mail me at: imboden@writing.org. I'll track down the new URL or let you know if the site appears to be dead and gone.

TIPS FOR SEARCHING ON YOUR OWN

The Web is vast, and you should regard the sites in this book as starting points for your own explorations. At some point, you'll want to try *Web indexes* and *search engines.*

Web Indexes

A Web index or directory is just what its name implies: a logically organized catalog of Web sites, arranged by topic and subtopic like the computer or card catalog at your public library. Two examples include Yahoo! and MiningCo.com.

Yahoo!

http://www.yahoo.com

The oldest Web index is still the largest, and its organization is rigid enough to satisfy the pickiest reference librarian. Unfortunately, travel seems to have been added as an afterthought. Some aspects of travel are under "Recreation and Sports," whereas destinations require drilling through the layers under "Regional." To make matters worse, Yahoo!'s links are frequently outdated. Still, Yahoo! has more links than any other index, so it's worth exploring when you're not in a hurry.

MiningCo.com

http://miningco.com

"We mine the Net so you don't have to," claim the 600-plus expert MiningCo. "guides," who edit topics like *Spas, Switzerland and Austria for Visitors,* and *Honeymoons* (see Figure 1–1). Each topic offers categorized and annotated Web links (e.g., "Venice Hotels— Historic Center") along with weekly or biweekly articles. Compared with Yahoo!, MiningCo.com has fewer categories and subcategories, but the topics that *are* covered have a greater depth of information and fewer broken links. Just as important, its travel sites are conveniently organized under subheadings like "Europe," "Resources," and "U.S./Canada." (*Note:* If you don't see a travel site listed for your destination, check http://miningco.com/local/ for listings of city and metro sites that usually have travel information.)

FIGURE 1-1

MiningCo.com.

The major search engines, which follow, often have indexes with directory headings such as "computers," "sports," and "travel." These tend to be skimpy at best, so stick with Yahoo! or MiningCo.com when you're in a mood for an index.

Search Engines

A search engine is a vast database of Web pages. Automated software robots, or spiders, routinely crawl the Web, gathering addresses, page titles, and keywords. Later, when you enter a term like "Paris hotels" into a query form, the search engine's software tries to find the most relevant pages from the millions that are stored in the database.

There are several problems with this approach:

- Computers aren't as smart as people, and the search engine may not realize that you mean Paris, France, rather than Paris, Texas, or that you're interested only in hotels within walking distance of the Louvre.
- Canny Web authors have been known to seed pages with false keywords, so that a user seeking information on the French capital may be propelled to a site where unclad couples are engaged in French kissing (and more).
- The Web is expanding at such a huge rate that the number of search hits, or results, can be overwhelming. (Search on the name "London," and the list of pages may run into the tens of thousands—possibly with an article on Jack London or the program of a January 1996 London symposium on nuclear fission ranking higher than the home page of the Tower of London or the London Tourist Board.)

Do these shortcomings make search engines worthless? No, but they do mean that search engines are most useful when:

- You're searching on a narrow topic, such as "Louvre Museum," rather than "Paris" or "French art."
- You know the individual search engine's quirks—e.g., whether a search on "Paris restaurants" will be interpreted as meaning pages with text that contains the word "Paris" *or* "restaurants," the words "Paris" *and* "restaurants," or the two-word phrase "Paris restaurants."

Fortunately, many search engines have advanced search options or allow Boolean searches, such as "Paris AND France AND restaurants OR bistros NOT McDonald's." To find out which choices are available for the search engine you're using, click the query page's Help or Advanced search link.

By now, you may be wondering which of the many search engines is likely to be most useful. Here are my personal recommendations:

AltaVista

http://www.altavista.com

This favorite of techies and serious researchers has fresher listings than most of its competitors. It even has a translator for Web pages. Newly submitted pages are added to the database within two or three days, rather than weeks or months. AltaVista also permits advanced searches that can winnow the hit list considerably. On the downside, a site with many similar pages may clutter up page after page of search results. If this happens, try:

Infoseek

http://infoseek.go.com

Infoseek's great strength is the relevancy of its hit lists. Search on the phrase "Venice Marco Polo Airport," and you're likely to find the home page for the airport in Venice, Italy, or my articles on that airport's boats and buses into the city. (Other search engines might give you a hodgepodge of listings for Venice's California and Florida namesakes, along with pages on the Italian explorer's voyages to the Far East.) Infoseek also groups multiple pages for the same Web site under one link, which makes it easier to scan your search results. However, its listings aren't always as fresh as AltaVista's.

If you're feeling adventurous after a few days with AltaVista and Infoseek, you may want to experiment with other search engines or with "metasearch" tools that query and pool results from many search engines automatically. For more information on advanced search techniques (and the foibles of individual search engines), see:

Web Search

http://websearch.miningco.com

Chris Sherman has assembled a vast collection of articles and Web links related to search engines, metasearch tools, Web directories, and search software.

Search Engine Watch

http://searchenginewatch.com

Danny Sullivan's site is popular with Web authors who use its technical information to improve the rankings of their pages in search engines, but it also has useful tips for advanced searchers.

2

CHAPTER

GETTING STARTED

Ready to plan your trip? Let's start by exploring basic travel resources on the Internet.

TRAVEL AGENCIES

Travel agencies come in two basic flavors: "storefront" and "on-line." At the storefront agency, you talk with a human being who recommends air fares, hotels, tour packages, makes the bookings for you, and so forth. At the on-line agency, you query a database and make your own bookings after you've examined the search results in your Web browser.

Which type of agency is best? There's no simple answer, but here are my recommendations:

- If you're simply buying airline tickets, it may be cheaper to book with an on-line agency. You'll avoid the nominal ticketing fees that many storefront agencies now charge, and—if you're patient—you may be able to find a better deal than an agent would. (Airlines keep cutting the commissions they pay to travel agents, and some fares—such as last-minute bargains on an airline's Web site—may not be commissionable.)

- If you're seeking a tour or cruise, see a local travel agent. Most tours and many cruises are marketed to the trade, and you're unlikely to find more than a small sampling of such packaged travel products on-line.
- If comparison shopping bores you and you don't have time for extensive research, use a local travel agent. The agent will appreciate the income, you'll be supporting a business in your community, and you'll avoid expensive mistakes.

For more information on travel agents, visit:

The American Society of Travel Agents (ASTA)

http://www.astanet.com/pub

ASTA has more than 26,500 member agencies in 165 countries, and you can search for local agencies by postal code. Also, you can complete an on-line Trip Request form, describing the trip you'd like to take. One or more ASTA agencies will respond with a suggested product or itinerary.

Even if you choose to work with a local travel agent, the on-line agencies are worth visiting to get an idea of what air fares and travel services may be available. Try these agencies first:

Atevo Travel

http://www.atevo.com

A. G. Dunham, Air Travel guide at MiningCo.com, calls this site "a must see and USE!" It isn't fancy to look at, but the reservations features work well, and the agency is good about answering e-mail from its customers. Plus, when you've returned from your trip, you can submit an article or create your own free travel Web page to describe your experiences.

Microsoft Expedia

http://expedia.msn.com

Expedia is one of the largest on-line travel agencies, and deservedly so. It's easy to use, it does a good job of finding low fares, and it sweetens the pot with features like a travel magazine, Web communities, and a "driving directions" tool for highway travelers (see Figure 2–1).

FIGURE 2–1

Microsoft Expedia.

Preview Travel

http://www.previewtravel.com

Visit Preview for its destination guides, which are supplied by Fodor's. The "Farefinder" tool is also handy: Select a departure airport, and it lists bargain fares to U.S. and international destinations.

Bestfares.com

http://www.bestfares.com

Discount air fares, air/land packages, and other special deals are featured on this site, which is operated by *Best Fares* magazine. Click "NewsDesk" for the latest flight bargains in coach and business class.

1Travel.com
http://www.1travel.com
Use the "Last Minute Deals" button to sign up for weekly e-mail that lists airfare, resort, and cruise bargains.

Priceline.com
http://www.priceline.com
Priceline lets you specify the maximum you're willing to pay for airline tickets, hotel rooms, and so on. If you're lucky, you'll get a bargain—but there are no guarantees.

GUIDEBOOK PUBLISHERS

Many Internet users regard the Web as a substitute for guidebooks. In reality, the Web and a good guidebook complement each other. Consider:

- The Web provides access to *primary resources,* such as hotel pages, official tourism sites, and transportation schedules. A hotel page, for example, may include photos of rooms, current rates, a map, and a reservations form.
- A guidebook provides *evaluations* of hotels, sights, and so on, based on the publisher's editorial criteria and standards. By comparing on-line promotional material with guidebook reviews, you can make better decisions when planning your trip.

Most guidebooks are available only in print; however, a number of guidebook publishers have put some of their content on their Web, hoping that you'll be tantalized into buying their books. Here are the publishers' sites worth visiting:

Fielding Worldwide
http://www.fieldingtravel.com
Fielding's "CruiseFinder" has ship reviews, while the "DangerFinder" is essential reading for adventure travelers.

Fodor's Travel Online
http://www.fodors.com
The hotel index, restaurant index, and resource center are worth a visit.

Arthur Frommer's Budget Travel Online

http://www.frommers.com

Click the "Destinations" link to read detailed travel information on 200 cities and islands that "accounts for more than 80 percent of all vacation travel."

The Insider's Guide

http://www.insiders.com

The full text of nearly 60 Insider's Guides to the United States and Bermuda is available on the Web at no cost.

Lonely Planet Online

http://www.lonelyplanet.com

Lonely Planet guidebooks represent excellent value, and its on-line destination guides are especially useful for travel in Latin America, Africa, and Asia.

Rick Steves' Europe Through the Back Door

http://www.ricksteves.com

Click "Country-by-Country Information" for excerpts from guidebooks by a TV travel guru and tour organizer.

Rough Guides

http://www.roughguides.com

The "Select a Guide" section has budget-travel advice and listings for more than 4000 destinations on six continents.

FREE BROCHURES

Travel brochures are available from many sources, but the easiest way to obtain them is from:

Worldwide Brochures

http://www.wwb.com

More than 15,000 free brochures, guides, and maps are available here. Search by destination or activity, select from the list of brochures displayed, and use the e-form to submit your order electronically.

MAPS

There's no substitute for a good printed map, but the Web offers a few goodies that you won't find in the rack at your local gas station. When you need an accordion-fold map of Timbuktu or a road atlas of Shangri-La, an on-line vendor can get it to you within a few days.

MapQuest

http://www.mapquest.com

Enter an address or zip code, and MapQuest will display a local map that you can zoom in on and print. Quick maps are also available; so are road directions within the United States.

How Far Is It?

http://www.indo.com/distance

Type in the names of two cities and click "Look it up!" to get the distance in miles and kilometers as the crow flies.

World Atlas and World Maps

http://geography.miningco.com/library/maps/blindex.htm

Matt Rosenberg's Geography site at MiningCo.com organizes Web maps and atlases by continent and region.

Elstead Maps

http://www.elstead.co.uk

This British firm's on-line catalog has more than 1500 pages of listings for maps, atlases, globes, gazeteers, route planners, and mapping software for the United Kingdom and other countries.

The Adventurous Traveler Bookstore: Maps

http://shop.gorp.com/atbook/maps.asp

Elstead has a much larger selection, but this U.S. company is a good alternative if you live in North America and need maps at the last minute.

PASSPORTS AND VISAS

If you're a U.S. or Canadian citizen and are traveling outside North America, you'll generally need a *passport*. This is a pocket-size booklet with ID information and a photo, and it's issued by your national government.

Obtaining a passport is fairly simple; the trickiest part for most people is obtaining a birth certificate or other acceptable proof of citizenship. Although the U.S. Passport Service claims to process passports in 25 days, you should allow six weeks (or, better yet, several months) during the busy spring and summer travel seasons.

When traveling, carry your passport in a neck pouch, zipped inside pocket, or other safe place. It's also a good idea to photocopy the page with your photo and ID information. Carry the copy separately from the passport, so you'll have proof of identity if your passport is lost or stolen.

In many countries, you'll be asked to leave your passport with the hotel desk for registration with the police. This is normal, providing you get it back within a few hours or overnight.

English-speaking travelers can obtain passports from the passport offices in their home countries:

U.S. Passport Services
http://travel.state.gov/passport_services.htm

Canada Passport Office
http://www.dfait-maeci.gc.ca/passport/passport.htm

U.K. Passport Agency
http://www.open.gov.uk/ukpass/ukpass.htm

Ireland Passports
http://www.irlgov.ie/iveagh/services/passports/passportfacilities.htm

Passports Australia
http://www.dfat.gov.au/passports

New Zealand Passports
http://inform.dia.govt.nz/internal_affairs/businesses/doni_pro/how2index.html

A *visa* is an endorsement on a passport by a foreign consulate, embassy, or immigration office. It gives the foreign traveler permission to visit the country for a specified period of time.

Some countries require visas of all travelers; others require visas only for students, for workers, or for tourists on long visits. For information on visa requirement, check the official tourist sites listed in the "Destinations" section of this book.

When you're in a hurry to get a passport, or if you don't live near a consulate or embassy of a country whose visa you need, try a commercial expediter. Here are two in the United States:

American Passport

http://www.americanpassport.com

This service will hand-carry your application to the National Passport Center and have a passport on its way to you within 24 hours.

Instant Passport

http://www.instantpassport.com

Visas are a specialty here; the company works with more than 100 consulates and offers expedited service for Brazil, China, India, and Russia.

PACKING

"How much should you pack?" is a question that inspires debate among experienced travelers. Some, like PBS travel guru Rick Steves, advocate traveling with nothing more than a lightweight nylon carry-on; others (the sort of people you see in the pages of *Condé Nast Traveler* magazine) wouldn't dream of leaving home without a matched, five-piece set of Louis Vuitton luggage.

In reality, the question of how much to pack (and what to pack it in) depends on the type of trip you're taking. If you're driving, the size of your vehicle's trunk will dictate your baggage allowance. If you're traveling by air, you need to ask yourself:

- "Will I be on the road constantly, or will I stay in one place?"
- "Can I afford taxis at my destinations, or will I have to take my luggage on the bus or subway?"
- "Will I be traveling cheaply and casually, or will I need to dress up for dinner every night?"
- "Am I built like Hulk Hogan, or am I a latter-day replica of Audrey Hepburn?"

Don't let yourself be bullied into underpacking, but don't make the mistake of carrying things you don't need, either. For more insights into packing, read:

Best Preparations: Packing for Travel

http://www.frommers.com/prep/pack/

Arthur Frommer offers tips on choosing and packing a suitcase, with warm- and cold-weather wardrobe lists.

The Travelite FAQ

http://members.tripod.com/~travelite/

Lani Teshima compares the pros and cons of different luggage types. Her packing suggestions include: "Save your holey socks and dingy underwear for your trip, and throw them away as you go!"

Packing for Europe

http://goeurope.miningco.com/library/weekly/aa980409.htm

This article (which I wrote) is geared toward travelers to Europe, but its suggestions work just as well in the United States and Canada.

HEALTH AND MEDICAL CARE

Illness and injuries can spoil a trip. At the very least, they can be nuisances—especially if you come down with an intestinal virus, whack your head, break a tooth, or require stitches shortly before a scheduled airline or ship departure. (At least one such incident happens in my family of five whenever we take a European trip.)

To some extent, you can avoid problems by using common sense. Don't brush your teeth with tap water if you're in a place where water should be boiled; don't gorge on spicy food if you have a sensitive stomach; don't walk up steeply angled sidewalks in Lisbon or San Francisco while wearing high-heeled shoes; if you're taking prescription drugs, keep duplicate bottles with you instead of packing them in checked luggage.

Two health-related Web sites are especially useful for travelers:

CDC Travel Information

http://www.cdc.gov/travel/travelmap.html

Get reliable, up-to-date advice on immunization requirements, epidemics, health risks, and staying well in 16 travel regions around the world.

IAMAT

http://www.sentex.net/~iamat/

The International Association for Medical Assistance to Travelers offers a directory of English-speaking physicians in 125 countries and territories who have agreed to treat IAMAT members.

SAFETY

Hijackings over the Atlantic, terrorism in Europe, bandit gangs in Mexico, and guerrilla attacks on tourists in Uganda are enough to make any tourist nervous. However, it's important to keep a sense of perspective. You're more likely to have your car stolen in Minneapolis than you are to be mugged in the back alleys of Venice. You have a better chance of being carjacked in Los Angeles than being hijacked on a flight between New York and Paris.

Common sense is the best defense wherever you travel. Would you walk through unfamiliar neighborhoods at night in your own city with a Gucci handbag or a brand-new camcorder dangling loosely from your shoulder? If your answer is no, don't do it in Chicago or Naples, either.

Still, there are places in the world where tourists risk greater dangers than they do in the typical American city. Two good sources of advice on travel dangers are:

Fielding's DangerFinder

http://www.fieldingtravel.com/df/

Fielding Travel's lively, well-written guide to *The Most Dangerous Places* tells how to avoid trouble in nasty or potentially scary spots around the world. It also provides some interesting statistics: for example, 42 percent of Europeans consider Florida dangerous, but only 7 percent are nervous about traveling in Turkey or Kenya.

U.S. State Department Travel Warnings and Consular Information Sheets

http://travel.state.gov/travel_warnings.html

The State Department issues travel warnings for countries in which there's an immediate danger to tourists. If you don't see a travel warning for a country you plan to visit, check the consular information sheets and scroll down to "Crime Information" for information on local crooks and scams. You may also want to read *A Safe Trip Abroad* at http://travel.state.gov/asafetripabroad.html, although some of its recommended precautions are more suited to ambassadors and CIA agents than ordinary tourists. (Sample advice: "As much as possible, plan to stay in larger hotels that have more elaborate security.")

TRAVEL INSURANCE

Homeowner's insurance doesn't always cover losses away from home. Your medical insurance or HMO coverage may not be honored by clinics and hospitals in distant locations. What if you have to cancel a prepaid cruise or package tour because of an emergency?

There's an easy answer: travel insurance. You can buy policies to cover lost or stolen baggage, medical emergencies, trip cancellations, trip delays, baggage delays, and losses resulting from a transportation carrier's bankruptcy. Your travel agent can arrange such coverage, or you can book a policy through:

> **Travel Guard International**
>
> http://www.travel-guard.com
>
> This company has been in business since 1982. It offers several levels of coverage for trips of up to 365 days. Although full coverage isn't cheap, it may be worth it if you're in a high-risk health category or have committed thousands of dollars to a trip.

MONEY AT HOME AND ABROAD

The first rule of money is "have enough." Beyond that, follow these tips to make the most of what you've got:

- **Use credit cards:** Visa and MasterCard are the most universal; American Express and Diners Club are favorites on the expense account circuit. Why use credit cards? Two reasons: Your potential losses from theft are minimal if you report a lost or stolen card promptly, and you'll get a better exchange rate overseas than you would with cash or traveler's checks.

  CAUTION: Some card issuers tack a charge of 2 or 3 percent, or more, onto foreign transactions. Such charges are in addition *to any fees that Visa or MasterCard charges for currency conversion. Before using a credit card overseas, call your issuer to learn what additional fees (if any) are levied on overseas purchases.*

- **Use ATM cards:** Bank automated teller machine (ATM) cards offer a quick, easy way to get local currency throughout the civilized world. They can also save you money if you're traveling outside your home country, because exchanges are computed at the bank wholesale rate, and transaction fees are nearly always lower than commissions at banks or exchange counters. (Exception: If you're traveling in countries in which black market exchanges are tolerated, cash may get you a better rate.)

  IMPORTANT: Many foreign ATM machines require four-digit numeric personal identification numbers (PINs), so ask your bank for a new number if yours doesn't meet that standard.

- **Carry traveler's checks:** For emergencies, a stash of $100 or $200 in traveler's checks can be handy. Buy a well-known brand like American Express or Thomas Cook, and follow the instructions for using them. (Issuers aren't required to replace lost or stolen checks if the traveler has been negligent.)

- **Exchange money abroad:** You'll pay a premium for changing money at the counter in your U.S. and Canadian airports, so wait to use the exchange counter or ATM at your destination, unless you're willing to pay extra for peace of mind.

MasterCard/Cirrus ATM Locator
http://www.mastercard.com/atm
Find an ATM by region or airport.

Visa/Plus ATM Locator
http://www.visa.com/cgi-bin/vee/pd/atm/main.html?2+0
This network has more than 457,000 ATMs in 120 countries.

Universal Currency Converter
http://www.xe.net/currency
Enter a number, select two currencies, and click the button (see Figure 2–2).

FIGURE 2–2

Universal Currency Converter.

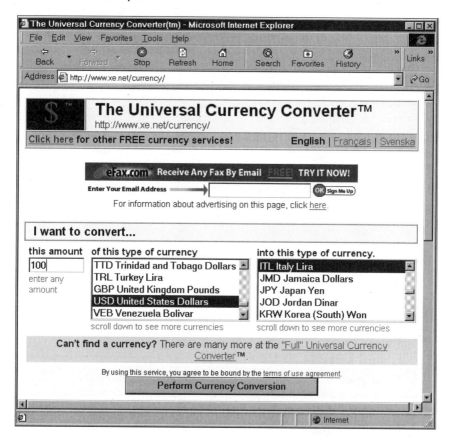

Foreign Currencies (with History Graphs)

http://www.x-rates.com

See what your local money is worth in 34 other currencies.
Graphs show trends over the last 7 to 120 days.

TIPPING

Tipping is always a tricky subject, with little general agreement on what separates a philanthropist from a cheapskate. My own philosophy is to tip generously unless there's a reason to do otherwise. An extra 5 percent won't drain my wallet, but a day's worth of extra quarters and dollars may mean the difference between steak and cornflakes for the recipient's family. For basic suggestions on tipping, see:

The Original Tipping Page

http://www.tipping.org

Manny Gonzales has researched tipping practices and offers general guidelines, plus links to other sites.

Tipping Customs Vary Worldwide

http://www.tastg.com/news/tipping.htm

The All Seasons Travel Group's page tells where to get a free booklet, entitled *Tips on Tipping,* from the American Society of Travel Agents.

National tourist offices and cruise lines frequently have tipping advice on their Web sites. (Some cruise lines even provide tip envelopes on board their ships.)

TIME ZONES

It's useful to know what time it is at your destination, especially when you're calling a hotel or resort in another time zone for reservations.

Burbs Time Zone Converter

http://www.burbs.com/fcgi-bin/tzconvert.fcgi

Enter your local time, pick your local and destination time zones, and click the button to learn what time it is in Texas or Taipei.

Time Zone Converter

http://www.timezoneconverter.com

This site is more complex than the one above, but it has extra bells and whistles—including a customized time zone reference card that you can print and take with you.

WEATHER AND CLIMATE

Should you pack an umbrella before leaving for Tulsa on Tuesday? What kind of wardrobe should you buy for a tour of Scandinavia in June? Here's where to find the answers:

Rain or Shine

http://www.rainorshine.com

Five-day forecasts give temperatures in Fahrenheit and Celsius. Click "Weather Cams" to see what's happening outside in 25 countries.

World Climate Weather

http://www.worldclimate.com

Enter a city name (using the local spelling) for a month-by-month summary of daily highs, lows, average temperatures, and rainfall.

CYBERTRAVEL

Getting connected and exchanging e-mail on the road is a big issue for many of today's wired travelers.

If you're traveling domestically and have an account with a national Internet service provider (ISP) like AOL, MSN, or AT&T WorldNet, finding connections should be easy. However, you may have to pay long-distance tolls when you're away from heavily populated areas.

Things get iffy when you're traveling overseas, because most domestic ISPs don't have foreign access numbers—and when they do, the dial-in points may be isolated and subject to high roaming fees.

Often, the simplest way to get connected is to visit a cybercafé where you can rent time on a computer. Then go to:

MailStart

http://www.mailstart.com

With MailStart, you can send, receive, and reply to mail at your regular POP3 (Internet mail) account back home just by entering your e-mail address and password on a Web page. It works beautifully—and it's free!

Of course, you'll need to find a cybercafé first, by consulting the index at:

The Cybercafé Search Engine

http://www.cybercaptive.com/bbs

The last time I checked, this database contained more than 2500 cybercafés and 2000 public Internet kiosks in 121 countries.

Finally, if you're taking your laptop abroad, be sure to check:

Help for World Travelers
http://kropla.com
International voltages, power plugs, phone jacks, and dialing codes are a few of the issues that Steve Kropla addresses with detailed text and drawings.

TRAVEL NEWSGROUPS

Long before the Web was invented, "Usenet newsgroups," or message boards, offered a way for Internet users to ask questions, get answers, and share opinions on-line. Newsgroups are still a great way to get free tips and comments from other travelers (see Figure 2–3). You can access them in two ways:

- **With a newsreader:** A "newsreader" is a program like Outlook Express (included with Microsoft Internet Explorer) or Collabra (part of Netscape Communicator). With it, you read messages ("articles" in Usenet lingo) and post your own messages or replies. For information on how to set up a newsreader with your ISP's "news server," consult the ISP's help page and the help file in your browser or newsreader program.
- **With DejaNews:** This is the simplest option if you're interested in a specific topic and don't plan to visit newsgroups regularly. Simply open your Web browser to http://www.dejanews.com and use the "Find" window to enter a topic like "Venice hotels" or "Caribbean cruises." Click the "Find" button, and you'll be given a list of messages on that topic from many different newsgroups. Or, you can select "Forums" instead of "Messages" for a list of suggested newsgroups. You can also post your own messages and replies with DejaNews without leaving your Web browser.

Usenet has many newsgroups for travelers, including:

alt.travel.eurail-hostels
alt.travel.road-trip
rec.travel.africa
rec.travel.air
rec.travel.asia

FIGURE 2–3

Newsgroups.

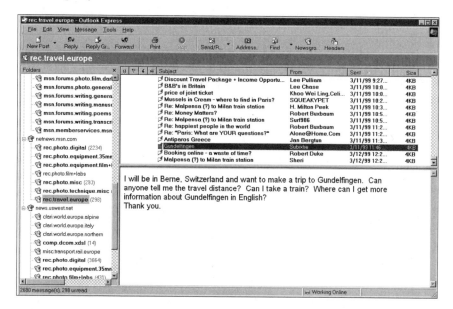

rec.travel.australia+nz

rec.travel.bed+breakfast

rec.travel.budget.backpack

rec.travel.caribbean

rec.travel.cruises

rec.travel.europe

rec.travel.latin-america

rec.travel.misc

rec.travel.resorts.all-inclusive

rec.travel.usa-canada

Newsgroup names tend to be self-explanatory, so—if you're using a newsreader—type a word like "travel" in the newsgroup search window and see what looks interesting. Also, don't be afraid to use the "subscribe" button in your newsreader if you want to visit a newsgroup in the future— "subscribing" means only that you're saving the newsgroup's address for future reference.

3

GETTING AROUND

AIR TRAVEL

General Information

Air Travel

http://airtravel.miningco.com

A. G. Dunham spent 12 years as a flight attendant, wrote for airline magazines, and flew more than 2 million miles to 39 countries before launching this consumer-oriented how-to site.

Rules of the Air

http://www.onetravel.com/rules/rules.cfm

Pick a U.S. airline and a topic (such as "oversold flights") to learn your rights in plain English or to read the published rule.

Airlines

Many airlines offer last-minute Internet fares and other special promotions on their Web sites. If you're flexible about departure dates and destinations, you can can get some great deals.

For a guide to nearly 500 airline Web sites, see:

Airlines of the World
http://flyaow.com
Click the "Airlines" icon for a directory of airline pages worldwide, or choose "Cyberfares" for links to special deals. You can also make reservations and look up airline or airport codes at AOW.

The Trip.com Flight Tracker
http://www.thetrip.com/usertools/flighttracking/0,1325,1-1,00.html
Enter an airline and flight number to check a plane's departure time, arrival time, and current location on a relief map.

Charters

Not so many years ago, charter airlines were a popular way to save money on flights to leisure destinations. Names like Condor and Martinair were synonymous with savings (and packed planes).

Charter airlines still exist, but the availability of cheap advanced-purchase fares and last-minute bargains on scheduled airlines makes the charter concept irrelevant for most North American travelers.

Consolidators

Consolidators, or "bucket shops," purchase discount tickets in bulk from the airlines and sell them at bargain prices. The fares are unpublished, meaning that the airlines won't tell you about them or sell you a ticket directly. For listings, see:

ETN Last-Minute Hotline Telephone Numbers
http://www.etn.nl/lastmin.htm
Call these agencies in the United States and the United Kingdom, or use the e-forms to request quotations. (ETN recommends phoning if you're flying at the last minute.)

Also visit Bestfares.com and check the "Newsdesk" at http://www.bestfares.com/newsdesk/newsdesk.htm for unadvertised or last-minute bargain fares. Don't forget the on-line travel agencies in the chapter entitled "Getting Started." Several of these will put you on e-mail lists for news of special fares on the routes that interest you.

Courier Companies

Courier services offer a cheap way to fly on short notice if you aren't carrying much luggage. In return for a subsidized airline ticket, you give up your allowance for checked baggage. The courier company then checks a suitcase of business documents to your destination under your name.

In most cases, you never touch the courier shipment. All you have to do is occupy a seat and give a manifest to the courier's agent upon arrival. The agent claims the suitcase while you catch the bus to your hotel.

Is this legal? Will you go to jail if the courier service hides a kilo of nose candy in that suitcase of business documents? For the answers, read the FAQ at:

IAATC Air Courier Travel

http://www.courier.org

The International Association of Air Travel Couriers explains how courier travel works. Members can check daily lists of available courier flights on the Web.

Frequent-Flier Programs

When American Airlines invented frequent-flier programs in 1982, the concept was simply a new twist on traditional "loyalty marketing" schemes like S & H Green Stamps and the Dunkin' Donuts punchcard. Today, such programs are one of the airline industry's most successful marketing tools—despite the fact that most passengers never accumulate enough miles to qualify for free travel.

To benefit from frequent-flier programs, you need to observe these simple but important rules:

1. **Pick an airline that you can use regularly.** If you live in a city or hub where one airline is dominant, use that airline whenever possible (all other things, including fares, being equal). If you have several major airlines to choose from, determine which airline has the most flights to places you're likely to visit.

2. **Pick the most generous frequent-flier program.** Look for a program with reasonable award goals, such as from 20,000 to 25,000 miles for an off-peak domestic ticket. Next, check the program's mileage expiration policy. (The better programs, such as Northwest's WorldPerks and Continental's OnePass, let you accrue miles indefinitely.)

3. **Look for alliances that match your travel interests.** Today more than ever, airlines are working together with code sharing and other marketing alliances. This makes it easier to rack up miles and claim awards while flying more than one airline. [Example: Delta lets you earn and redeem SkyMiles on 14 international airlines (subject to various exclusions). This makes SkyMiles a good bet if you live near a Delta hub and plan to travel overseas.]

4. **Check the fine print.** International partners of U.S. airlines may not award miles for discount fares. This means you could fly from Tupelo to Paris and earn credit only for the Tupelo–New York leg of your trip. If that's the case, you may want to fly on another airline that awards full mileage to discount travelers, assuming that you can get a comparable fare.

5. **Take advantage of non–airline partner offers, but don't be obsessive.** Credit cards, long-distance phone services, car rental firms, and hotel chains are just a few of the businesses that award frequent-flier miles. If such partners offer the services you need at competitive prices, then by all means use them. But remember: An overpriced hotel or a credit card with a 1.75 percent monthly finance charge is no bargain, even if it does reward you with frequent-flyer miles.

To read the Web's most detailed advice on frequent-flier programs, go to:

WebFlyer
http://www.webflyer.com
Randy Peterson has been tracking frequent-flier programs since the mid-1980s, when he started *InsideFlyer* magazine. His WebFlyer site has reviews of frequent-flier programs, news of bonus awards, and a form that lets you enroll in up to five airline programs with a single click.

BUS TRAVEL

Ever since I took a three-day bus trip from Los Angeles to New York at the age of 18, I've had an aversion to bus travel in any form. Still, millions of people around the world ride buses happily every day, and who am I to question their wisdom?

For the ultimate compendium of information on bus travel, open your Web browser to:

Routes International: Bus Sites

http://www.routesinternational.com/buslines.htm

This page has links to scores of bus sites, intercity bus lines, and charter lines on six continents.

United States/Canada

Greyhound Lines

http://www.greyhound.com

"Take the bus and leave the driving to us," says America's only nationwide bus carrier.

Greyhound Canada

http://www.greyhound.ca

Schedule a trip on-line, or download timetables in Adobe Acrobat format to print and take along.

United Motorcoach Association

http://www.uma.org

Use the searchable database to locate 850-plus scheduled carriers and charter-bus operators throughout the United States.

Europe

Busabout

http://www.busabout.com

The Busabout network offers low-cost transportation to 60 European cities. An affiliated Bedabout program offers cheap bungalow accommodations or hotel vouchers.

Bus Éirann

http://www.buseireann.ie

Irish bus lines outside Dublin are covered here.

Eurobus

http://www.frugaltraveler.com/eurobusmain.htm

From June to October, Eurobus operates coaches on three European circuits plus a daily link between London and Paris.

Eurolines

http://www.eurolines.traveltv.net/eurolini/ruta_reg.htm

Eight European countries and Morocco are linked to Spain via Eurolines España.

National Express

http://www.nationalexpress.co.uk

This company bills itself as "the United Kingdom's only national bus and coach travel network."

Scottish CityLink

http://www.citylink.co.uk

Check timetables and fares for bus routes between Glasgow and Edinburgh, on the West Coast, and in northern Scotland.

Australia

Australian Bus Lines

http://www.buslines.com.au

This massive site has listings and links for intercity, local, and charter lines throughout the country, with a few tram and rail lines tossed in for good measure.

Adventure Bus Tours

The ANT

http://www.theant.com

"The ultimate hop-on/hop-off backpacker travel network" operates two bus loops in California, Arizona, Nevada, and New Mexico. An ANT pass is good for six months.

Green Tortoise

http://www.greentortoise.com

Buses with bunk beds and "millions of miles of character" carry tour members to Alaska, Death Valley, New Orleans, Costa Rica, and other destinations in North and Central America.

Sightseeing Excursions

Gray Line Worldwide

http://www.grayline.com

Gray Line's headquarters Web site describes bus sightseeing tours in 200 American and foreign destinations. Also see Grey Line Canada at http://www.greyhound.ca.

CAR TRAVEL

In the United States and Canada, driving is still the most popular form of travel. Many Americans and Canadians have never flown, and even fewer have traveled by railroad or ship.

Car travel has three big advantages over other modes of transportation: it's convenient, familiar, and cheap. For the price of a one-way airline ticket between Minneapolis and Milwaukee, you can buy enough gas to drive your automobile across the country and back. Even if you do fly, you'll probably want a car when you reach your destination, unless you're staying in the heart of an urban city like New York, Boston, Chicago, or San Francisco.

When to Rent a Car

Taking your own car becomes less attractive with each additional day of driving time. If you live in Indianapolis and you're headed for the Colorado Rockies, driving will take a day and a half each way—time that could be spent fishing for trout or spraining your ankle on the ski slopes. If you can afford it, leave your car in the garage and fly to Denver, then rent a car to your destination.

Owners of small cars or older vehicles may want to consider renting a large sedan or minivan before hauling the spouse and kids on an extended vacation. Packing a week's worth of vacation gear into the trunk may be a necessity, not a luxury, and not having to worry about a defunct water pump in the Nevada desert is worth the price of a rental.

Domestic Car Rentals

For rentals in the United States and Canada, it's easy enough to pick up your local Yellow Pages and call the national toll-free numbers for any major firm. Avis, Budget, Hertz, National, and other major companies have branches all over; so do many second-tier firms like Alamo and Enterprise.

If you'd rather not disconnect your modem to make a phone call, try these Web sites:

Breezenet's Guide to Airport Rental Cars

http://www.bnm.com

Pick an airport and click the car rental links to check rates or make reservations. Be sure to read the "Car Rental Tips" and "Rental FAQs," which can help you avoid mistakes and save money.

TravelSeeker: Car Agencies

http://travelseeker.com/rental.htm

This page has links to major rental firms in the United States and Europe.

National Car Rental

http://www.nationalcar.com

My own favorite domestic rent-a-car company scores high in *Consumer Reports* reviews, and its prices tend to be competitive with other major brands.

Overseas Car Rentals

Many of the companies that rent in the United States and Canada have agencies in other countries. However, rental rates and legal requirements may be different in Brussels than they are in Boston, so comparison shop before you make a reservation.

Can you handle a manual transmission? Automatic transmissions are usually limited to higher-priced cars outside North America, so you'll save greatly on rental fees if you're willing to use a shift lever and clutch.

Finally, if you're visiting Europe for a month or more, look into car leasing and buyback plans.

Major overseas rental firms include:

Europcar

http://www.europcar.com

Don't let the name mislead you: Europcar rents not only in Europe, but also in Africa, the Mideast, India, and French overseas territories.

Europe by Car

http://www.europebycar.com

Besides renting and leasing cars, this 45-year-old company will sell you an International Driving Permit. It has toll-free numbers within the United States.

Kemwel Holiday Autos

http://www.kemwel.com

The Wellner family has owned the Kemwel Group since 1908. This British company offers rentals, leases, and chauffeur-driven cars around the world.

Insurance

Car insurance policies in the United States are generally good in Canada, and vice versa, but check with your insurance company before crossing the border. In other countries, such as Mexico, you'll have to buy a local policy. Mexican policies are available at the border or from Sanborn's at:

http://www.xanadu2.net/sanborns-laferia/

When you rent a car, you'll be offered a Collision Damage Waiver (CDW) that can cost anywhere from $5 to $20 or more a day. Within the United States and Canada, you can safely decline the CDW option under the following circumstances:

- Your private or company insurance covers rental cars. (If you aren't sure, ask your insurance agent.)
- Your credit card includes free CDW coverage. (American Express, Diners Club, and gold or platinum Visa and MasterCards should, but check in case your card issuer's policy has changed.)

The rules are often different overseas:

- In some countries, such as Italy, you may be required to take CDW coverage.
- In other countries, the agency may place a "hold" of several thousand dollars on your credit card unless you accept the CDW option. If you get into an accident, the rental firm will charge the repairs to your account, and you'll have to seek reimbursement from your free CDW provider (e.g., your gold- or platinum-card issuer) after you get home. It may be wisest to take the CDW coverage so a fender bender won't spoil your trip.

Finally, if you reject CDW coverage, make sure that you won't be responsible for "administrative fees" above the cost of repairs. These can total several hundred dollars, and the money will have to come out of your pocket if your insurance doesn't cover them.

Directions

AutoPilot

http://www.freetrip.com

Enter a starting city or destination in the United States and Canada, along with your preference for types of roads and accommodations. AutoPilot will generate a detailed itinerary with road directions, hotels, and service plazas. It will even tell you the total distance, time elapsed, and time remaining at each checkpoint along the way.

DeLorme CyberRouter

http://www.delorme.com/cybermaps/route.asp

DeLorme, a publisher of mapping software and atlases, offers free on-line driving itineraries with AAA maps in two different styles.

Rand McNally Online: Road Construction

http://www.randmcnally.com/construction/

Select a state or province for a list of current road projects to avoid while driving.

EuroShell Route Planner

http://www.euroshell.com/base_routeue.html

This site can be slow to load, but it lets you generate English-language road directions and maps for Europe. Shell stations are listed in each itinerary.

Speed Traps

The Speedtrap Registry

http://www.speedtrap.com

If you drive with a heavy foot, check this list of U.S. and overseas readers' reports before you risk a ticket.

International Driving

Driving overseas can be a nerve-racking experience for U.S. and Candian motorists, especially in countries like Mexico and Italy where traffic may be heavier and drivers more aggressive than they are in a city like Ottawa or Des Moines.

Driving on the left (as in Britain, Ireland, and Australia) is another challenge that can leave foreign motorists wishing they'd stuck with public transportation.

Before driving abroad, study these Web sites:

General Comments on the European Traffic Code

http://www.travlang.com/signs

This site is a visual nightmare, but the information is helpful. Links take you to pages with international traffic signs that you'll see in many regions, not just Europe.

Moto-Europa

http://www.ideamerge.com/motoeuropa/

Click the "Chapters" link for exhaustive information on driving in Europe. You can also rent a vehicle, buy insurance, or line up a traveling companion on the rideshare board.

Visiting Britain: Car Hire and Travel

http://www.soon.org.uk/britcart.htm

Rules, tips, and a plug for the invaluable London Parking Guide are available here.

Campers and Motorhomes

Traveling with recreational vehicles is a topic that deserves a book of its own—and, in fact, you'll discover quite a few such books if you search your local bookstore or Amazon.com. Instead of pretending to be an expert on RV travel, I'll refer you to people who are:

RVers Online

http://www.rversonline.org

Travelogs describe RV drivers' experiences in the United States and Canada, and there's a large collection of articles on RV travel in Mexico.

RV Zone

http://www.rvzone.com

This site lists campgrounds that accept RVs, rental firms, service centers, RV travel Web sites for specific regions, and more.

CampNet America

http://www.campnetamerica.com

The "Campground Locator" lists RV parks in the United States, Canada, Europe, and Australia, with more to come.

Motorhome, Camper, and Van Links—Europe

http://goeurope.miningco.com/msub-motorhome.htm

Use this page to find general information and rental agencies in Europe. Also, be sure to read *Europe by Motorhome and Van,* a book featured on the page.

RAIL TRAVEL

The heyday of rail travel in North America is long gone, but trains are still a popular form of transportation in many other parts of the world. And no wonder: With speeds that approach 200 mph and stations located conveniently in city centers, modern railroads put airlines and interstate highways to shame for trips of under 500 miles.

United States/Canada

In the United States and Canada, intercity rail travel falls into two categories:

- Business/commuter travel, with frequent service on routes such as Washington–New York–Boston and San Diego–Los Angeles
- Leisure travel, often following routes that were pioneered by classic trains like the Super Chief and the Empire Builder

Rail travel isn't necessarily cheap. In fact, a coach ticket on Amtrak between New York and Miami may cost more than an excursion airfare— and that's without a sleeping berth, which can cost hundreds of dollars more.

Still, rail travel does offer certain advantages: It allows sightseeing; it's faster than driving on long trips; and it's a new experience for many travelers. If you think of a rail trip as a cruise, not as a means of transportation, the price isn't so bad.

A few tips:

- Ask about discounts and special packages. Off-season reductions are common, and Amtrak has a "Rail Sale" page on its Web site that offers savings of up to 90 percent on last-minute ticket purchases.
- To avoid backtracking, buy an Amtrak Air Rail package, which combines a rail trip with a one-way flight on United Airlines.
- Compare ticket prices carefully on routes in the Northeast. The high-speed Metroliner trains may not save you enough time to justify their high ticket prices unless your employer is footing the bill.

Amtrak

http://www.amtrak.com

America's National Railroad Passenger Corporation has had its ups and downs over the years, but for most Americans it's the only train game in town.

VIA Rail Canada

http://www.viarail.ca

Canada's passenger lines run from Nova Scotia and the Gaspé Peninsula to British Columbia, with a route extending north from Winnipeg to Hudson Bay.

TrainWeb

http://trainweb.com

This site is loaded with articles and links for travelers and railfans, with an emphasis on North America.

Europe

In Europe, trains are often the quickest way to get from city to city. Many European railroads are adding services at a time when North American railroads are cutting back. A good example is the new Eurostar, which uses the English Channel Tunnel to connect Paris and London in three hours. (New track and local tunnels will shave another 25 minutes off that time by 2003.)

Most European railways are government owned, with notable exceptions in a few countries like Britain (which has sliced British Rail into 26 private companies) and Switzerland (where the Swiss Federal Railways and many smaller private railroads are integrated seamlessly into a national transportation network of trains, buses, lake and river steamers, finiculars, cable cars, and chairlifts). Even in countries where a trip may involve travel on two or three different railroads, you can plan your itinerary with a common timetable and buy a ticket for your entire journey at any railroad station or travel agency. The same rule applies to trips involving railroads in several European countries.

What's the cheapest way to travel by rail in Europe? Let's examine three possibilities.

European Rail Passes

Eurail Pass is the best-known option in this category; the standard pass provides unlimited first-class travel in 17 European countries for periods that range from 15 days to 3 months. Variations such as the Eurail Youth Pass are also available.

Europass is a newer option. It includes 5 days of travel in five "base" countries (France, Germany, Italy, Switzerland, and Spain) plus one or more "associate" countries, with up to 10 more travel days available at extra cost.

Other possibilities include rail/drive passes that let you take the train between major destinations and use rental cars for local excursions.

Pro: Eurail Pass and Europass are easy to use, and they're cost-effective if you plan to cover a lot of territory by train.

Con: You're paying a premium for first-class travel (which is overkill on most routes), and discounts on some services may be less than you'd get with a national rail pass.

National Rail Passes

These should be called "transportation passes" instead of "rail passes," because in some countries—such as Switzerland—they include unlimited travel by train, bus, boat, and local public transit, with steep discounts on private railways, funiculars, cable cars, and chairlifts.

Pro: If most of your trip will be spent in one or two countries, a national rail pass is likely to be a far better value than Eurail Pass or Europass.

Con: You'll need more than one rail pass (or you'll need a rail pass plus point-to-point tickets) when you visit more than one country.

Point-to-Point Tickets

Trips over limited distances or between just a few cities may be cheaper when you buy standard rail tickets. Local discounts for family travel, day excursions, and so forth, can also make point-to-point tickets a better deal than rail passes.

Pro: You pay for what you use.

Con: You may find yourself struggling with a foreign language while a dozen local commuters line up behind you at the ticket counter. (The antidote, if that happens, is to buy your tickets at a local travel agency where the staff speaks English.)

For more information on European rail travel, or to buy passes and tickets ahead of time, visit these Web sites:

Europrail International

http://www.eurail.on.ca

Design your own Europass, buy Eurail products, or purchase national passes. Free on-line maps and schedules are also available.

Rail Europe

http://www.raileurope.com/us

This subsidiary of the French and Swiss national railroads sells passes and tickets for 60 European railways. Its FAQ answers the most common questions about rail travel in Europe.

Rick's Railpass Guide

http://www.ricksteves.com/rail

Rick Steves, *Europe by the Back Door* author and TV host, sells rail passes in his spare time. His "rail pass worksheet" helps you decide what kind of pass to buy.

FIGURE 3–1

SBB Travel Online.

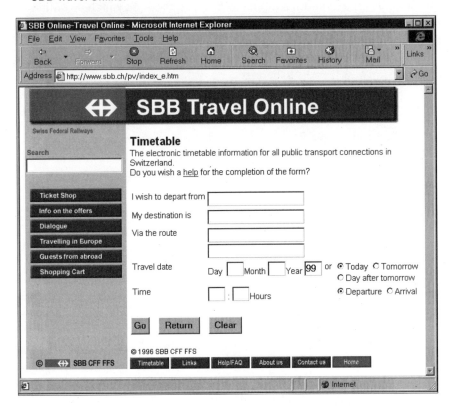

SBB Travel Online

http://www.sbb.ch/pv/index_e.htm

The Swiss Federal Railway offers a streamlined timetable for connections throughout Europe (see Figure 3–1).

Eurostar

http://www.eurostar.co.uk

Travel in style from London to Paris or Brussels in less time than it takes to watch *Titanic*.

Railtrack

http://www.railtrack.co.uk/travel/

Plan a rail trip in Britain with an on-line query form.

European Rail Timetables

http://goeurope.miningco.com/library/weekly/aa990114.htm

This collection of annotated links points to local journey planners and home pages for 17 European countries.

Rail Travel in Other Countries

RailServe

http://www.railserve.com

Click the menu window and scroll to the "Passenger and Urban Transit" listings for railway pages and timetables on six continents.

SHIP TRAVEL

If you've never traveled by ship, you're missing a treat. As a pre–baby boomer, I can remember the waning days of ocean liners when the *Queen Mary, Queen Elizabeth, France, Bremen, Michelangelo, Raffaelo, Cristoforo Columbo, Rotterdam, Constitution, Independence,* and a dozen others lined up like cars in parking slots on the West Side of Manhattan every week. Those days are gone; the *Queen Mary* is now a hotel, the *France* is a Norwegian cruise ship, the *Mikhail Lermontov* sank off New Zealand a few years after carrying me to Bremerhaven, and most of the other great liners have been recycled into cars or razor blades. However, you can still travel by ship—and you should, if you've never had the opportunity.

Cruises

Most of today's passenger ships are cruisers, not ocean liners. A cruise differs from an ocean passage in being a circular tour instead of a point-to-point crossing. The travel experience becomes the purpose of the trip, rather than merely being an enjoyable means to an end.

The word "cruise" is typically associated with the Caribbean, if only because so many cruise itineraries focus on that warm and sunny region. However, you can find cruises to just about anywhere: the Baltic in summer, the Mediterranean in spring, the Panama Canal, Alaska, the South Pacific, Antarctica, or around the world.

What's more, cruises come in an amazing variety of price ranges: from cheap three-day trips for the mass market to cruises that last several months and cost $20,000 or more. Theme cruises are increasingly popular, too: look hard enough, and you'll find cruises for jazz fans, chamber musicians, wildlife enthusiasts, and the corporate incentive market.

Rather than try to list all cruise lines here (and leave something else out of the book), I'll point you to Web sites that have everything you need to know about cruise lines and their ships:

Cruises

http://cruises.miningco.com

Linda Coffman serves up a veritable midnight buffet of articles and Web links for cruise fans, including pointers to other cruising guides.

Fielding's Cruise Finder

http://www.fieldingtravel.com/cf/

The quantity of information here is enormous. Select a cruise line, then examine capsule reports in 16 categories, such as "who should go," "who should not go," "bill of fare," and "gimmicks." You can also read reviews of individual ships and search for a cruise by region, rating level, and "best" lists.

The Industry of Cruising

http://www.frommers.com/standard/cruising/

The title sounds like a *Fortune* article, but Arthur Frommer's guide to cruising has everything from "outspoken appraisals" of 81 ships to advice on cargo liners.

Ferries

Passenger/car ferries are today's counterparts to the second-tier, bread-and-butter ocean liners of a generation ago. Most are comfortable, and the better European ships often have luxury touches, such as cabins with beds (rather than the usual bunks) and white-tablecloth restaurants.

Australia

Spirit of Tasmania

http://www.tt-line.com.au

Book anything from a hostel berth to a suite, and pick from three restaurants during the overnight crossing between Melbourne and Devonport.

FIGURE 3–2

Alaska Marine Highway.

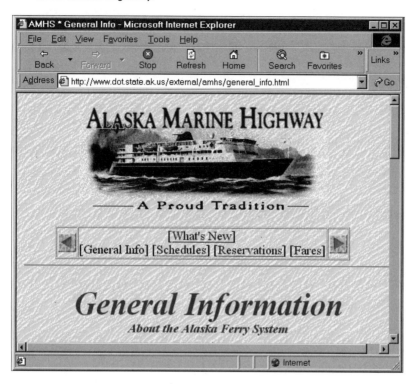

North America

Alaska Marine Highway System

http://www.dot.state.ak.us/external/amhs/home.html

Ferries connect Alaska's coastal communities with each other and
the Lower 48. Accommodations range from cabins to compartments
with airline seating, and the public spaces tend to be crowded in
summer (see Figure 3–2).

BC Ferries

http://www.bcferries.bc.ca/

Many of these vessels are on short-haul routes, but dayrooms and
overnight cabins are available on the Inside Passage cruise.

Lake Michigan Carferry

http://www.ssbadger.com

The SS *Badger* doesn't really belong in these listings, because the crossing from Manitowoc to Ludington takes only a few hours and there are no cabins. Still, by Midwestern standards, it's a worthy rival to the *QE2*. (For a history of Lake Michigan ferries, see http://www.execpc.com/~abuelow/ferry.html.)

Marine Atlantique

http://www.marine-atlantic.ca/introe.html

Two 1200-passenger car ferries, the *Caribou* and *Smallwood,* run between Newfoundland ports and North Sydney, Nova Scotia. Cabins and dormitory sleepers are available on both ships, with "daynighter" seats being a cheaper option on the *Smallwood.*

Europe

Overnight "ferryliners" are legion in Europe. Routes include:

- Denmark to the Faroes, Norway, Iceland, and Shetlands
- England to Holland, Denmark, Norway, Sweden, and Spain
- Ireland to France
- Italy to Greece
- Norwegian North Cape
- Spain (mainland) to the Balearics and Canaries

and too many other routes to mention here.

For the Web's most complete set of links to European ferry sites, see:

European Ferries

http://goeurope.miningco.com/msub-ferries.htm

This entry page leads to collections of ferry links for the English Channel and Irish Sea, Northern Europe, and Southern Europe.

My personal recommendations for European ferry journeys include:

Scandinavian Seaways

http://www.scansea.com

Book a cabin or couchette from Harwich or Newcastle, England, to one of this first-rate Danish company's Scandinavian or German destinations. (The line also runs a convenient overnight ferry between Copenhagen and Oslo.) Minicruises are available, and the Harwich office's ship/land holiday packages are fantastic deals.

Smyril Line

http://www.smyril-line.fo

The M/F *Norröna*'s weekly sailings include stops in Denmark, the Faroe Islands, the Shetlands, Western Norway, and Eastern Iceland. If you have just a week, sail from Hanstholm to Tórshavn. Spend two nights in the Faroes, then rejoin the ship for the round-trip to Iceland and the return to Denmark.

Passenger Liners

Today, only one ship qualifies as a transoceanic passenger liner: the *Queen Elizabeth 2*. During the winter, the 30-year-old *QE2* sails around the world, but it returns to the North Atlantic route in April for a series of 15 or more six-day crossings between Southhampton, England, and New York. Bring your tuxedo or cocktail dress and a few thousand dollars for a stateroom. The ship is owned and operated by Cunard Line, http://www.cunardline.com.

Freighters

Freighter travel has declined in popularity over the last few decades, not for lack of passengers, but rather because of a dwindling number of ships that offer passenger accommodations. This doesn't mean you can't travel by freighter; it just means you have to plan ahead by visiting Web sites like these:

Internet Guide to Freighter Travel

http://members.aol.com/CruiseAZ/freighters.htm

R. F. Ahern is an inveterate freighter traveler. His site tells where to find a freighter agent, how to arrange a trip, and what to expect on board.

Freighter World Cruises

http://www.freighterworld.com

Use the "Destinations" page to select routes from an interactive world map.

Maris Freighter-Cruises.com

http://www.cruisemaris.com

Maris offers an FAQ, a monthly newsletter by subscription, and descriptions of freighter trips that can be reserved by calling the agency's toll-free number in New York.

TravLTips Freighter Cruise & Travel

http://travltips.com

Click the "Freighter Directory" button for listings of shipping lines, some with Web links.

The Cruise People Ltd.

http://members.aol.com/CruiseAZ/freighters.htm

This Canadian agency has offices in Toronto and London, and its home page has links to many freighter companies that carry passengers.

Finally, I can't resist plugging what may be the only remaining U.S.-flag cruise line:

American Hawaii Cruises

http://www.cruisehawaii.com

In the late 1960s, I traveled the American Export Lines route between Italy and New York on the SS *Independence.* Today, this refurbished 1951-vintage ocean liner is owned by American Hawaii Cruises, which offers seven-day cruises between Oahu, Kauai, Maui, and Hawaii year-round.

Barges and Canal Boats

In Britain and Continental Europe, converted freight barges offer cruises on nineteenth-century canals. At night, when the barges are moored, passengers can explore local villages and towpaths.

Boat rentals are also available in many places, with vessels ranging from modern fiberglass cabin cruisers to refitted wooden narrow boats.

Many companies offer cruises and rentals; here are a few URLs to whet your interest:

Abercrombie & Kent

http://www.signaturetravel.com/barge.htm

Three barges carry from 6 to 24 passengers on French canals. In addition to three- and six-day cruises, family charters are available.

Afloat in France

http://www.bargeaif.com

"Luxury" is the keyword here. Amenities include candlelit dinners, fine wines, an air-conditioned minivan for local sightseeing, and a first-class TGV train ticket for your return to Paris.

Crown Blue Line

http://www.bcomm.co.uk/oldcrown/english/eindex.htm

Select from more than 400 modern boats that you pilot yourself in France or Holland.

European Waterways

http://www.europeanwaterways.com

Six- to 12-passenger barges cruise through the countryside of England, France, Holland, and Ireland. Cruises include guided tours of local historic and cultural sights.

Self-Drive Barges

http://www.fieldingtravel.com/cf/altcruis/canalbrg/selfdriv.htm

Fielding's CruiseFinder tells where to rent U-drive boats in Britain, France, and Holland.

River Cruises

Cruise World

http://www.cruiseworld.com/RIV.HTM

This U.S. agency represents river cruise lines in the United States, Austria, France, Germany, Egypt, and Russia.

Delta Queen Steamboat Company

http://www.deltaqueen.com

Cruise the Mississippi, the Ohio, and nine other rivers aboard the *Delta Queen, American Queen,* and *River Queen.*

KD River Cruises

http://rivercruises.com/explore.htm

Cruise the Rhine, Elbe, Moselle, Danube, and other rivers in France, Germany, Austria, and Hungary.

Peter Deilmann EuropAmerica Cruises

http://www.deilmann-cruises.com/

More than 180 European river itineraries on five deluxe boats are available from this German firm. The Web site has timetables, deckplans, and sample daily programs.

RiverBarge Excursions

http://rivercruises.com

Tour seven regions in the American South aboard the R/B *River Explorer,* which is pushed by a towboat and looks like a steamboat without paddles.

Other Boat Charters

Houseboats, sailboats, and motor yachts are available from thousands of charter firms, and the easiest way to find a charter is to check the tourism sites listed in the "Destinations" section. Here are a few listings just to whet your boating appetite:

Houseboat Rental Directory

http://www.houseboat.net/houseboat_rentals.html

The Houseboating Guide's rental listings include firms in 37 states and 7 Canadian provinces.

Caribbean On-Line: Sailing, Yachting, & Boat Charters

http://www.caribbean-on-line.com/sailing/

The six companies here offer bareboats and crewed yachts throughout the Caribbean.

Charter Yachts in Greece

http://www.gfas.com/greekcharters/

Motor yachts, motor sailers, and sailing yachts are available bare or with crews. Click on the boat photos for specifications and charter rates.

World Wide Sail

http://www.duhe.com

Click the interactive map for links to charter services on five continents plus the Caribbean.

4

CHAPTER

GETTING SETTLED

At my Europe for Visitors site, pages of hotel links draw more traffic than just about anything else. There's obviously something in the human psyche that makes nearly all of us crave a home away from home. It's a bit ironic that we often spend most of our travel budgets on rooms that isolate us from the places we're paying to visit.

HOTELS/RESORTS

There's nothing new about the challenge of finding a place to stay. After all, Jesus was born in a manger because Joseph and Mary couldn't book a room at the inn ahead of time with an 800 number.

In the "Destinations" section, you'll find hotel and resort lists at most official and commercial tourism sites. Hotel Web pages typically list rates and special promotions. Usually, there's an e-form or e-mail address that you can use to obtain more information or exercise your chutzpah by asking about unadvertised deals.

The on-line travel agencies in the "Getting Started" section also handle room reservations. If you're in a hurry, try one of these specialized search engines:

All Hotels on the Web

http://www.all-hotels.com

The name may be hyperbole, but the database *does* include hotels from Greenland to Tahiti and most places in between.

ResortsandLodges.com

http://www.resortsandlodges.com

Search for a resort by type, location, or activity—for example, archaeology/anthropology, dude ranches, naturist resorts, or casinos.

Resorts Online

http://www.resortsonline.com

Pick a category such as "skiing" or "beach," then select a region for a list of resorts with Web links.

TravelWeb

http://www.travelweb.com

Need a room in Arkansas or Albania? Click the "hotel search" link, then complete the form for a list of hotels with photos, rates, and other information.

For an eclectic library of resort articles and Web links, see:

Elegant Hotels, Resorts, and Inns

http://elegantresorts.miningco.com

Jána Jones can point you to ecoresorts, golf resorts, couples-only resorts, and the "weird, wild, and obscure," such Jules' Undersea Lodge in Florida and the Ice Hotel in Kiruna, Sweden (Figure 4–1).

BED-AND-BREAKFASTS

The term "B&B" is elastic. It can refer to a romantic, antique-filled inn on the National Register of Historic Places, a private home with rooms for rent, or a down-at-the-heels guesthouse with a flair for marketing. The phrase "caveat emptor" comes to mind when shopping for a B&B, because private ownership and hands-on management don't necessarily translate into quality.

FIGURE 4–1

Ice Hotel, Kiruna, Sweden.

On the rocks: At the hotel's bar it's the same as "straight-up" because the glasses themselves are ice.

The more you know about a B&B, the more comfortable you can feel about making a reservation. Here are three Web sites that can point you to the information you need:

American Bed & Breakfast Association

http://www.abba.com

Click on "Find a B&B or inn," then select a state for listings of establishments that have been inspected and rated by the AB&BA.

Bed & Breakfasts

http://bandb.miningco.com

Erik and Elizabeth Arneson have assembled nearly 40 pages of annotated links to B&B Web sites, together with weekly or biweekly articles dating back to 1997. Some of the more intriguing categories include B&Bs that supply guests with cats, inns where you'll find "a ghost in addition to a host," and bed-and-breakfasts where horses are allowed (though presumably not in the rooms).

The Innkeeper's Register

http://www.innbook.com

The 345 inns and B&Bs in the Independent Innkeepers' Association directory have been ranked after at least one night's stay by an evaluator using the standards in Norman Simpson's *Country Inns and Back Roads.*

APARTMENT, VILLA, AND COTTAGE RENTALS

If you're staying at your destination for a week or more, why not set up housekeeping in a furnished apartment, cottage, or villa? You could save money over the cost of a hotel, especially if your family is large enough to need more than one room.

Over the years, my family and I have enjoyed the self-catering life in cities and rural areas of California, Austria, Denmark, Germany, and Switzerland. As I write this, we're about to spend two weeks in a three-bedroom apartment with garden near Venice's Frari church. The cost: just over $1000 a week, or roughly the price of a double room with breakfast in a three-star hotel.

Saving money, however, is only one reason to rent an apartment, villa, chalet, or cottage. With your own place, you're likely to have a kitchen in which you can eat or drink at any hour of the day or night without calling room service. You may have a washing machine so you can do your laundry. Furthermore, you can enjoy the fantasy of living in another place instead of just passing through.

Finding a rental can be more complicated than locating a hotel, because most travel agencies and guidebooks don't list them. If you know your destination, try the local tourist office or its Web site. Otherwise, one of these sources may be helpful:

1001 Villa Holiday Lets

http://www.1001-villa-holidaylets.com

Use the search window to pick a country and region, then view photos and descriptions of available rentals. Bookings are made directly with the property owners.

Barclayweb

http://www.barclayweb.com

This upmarket company has offices in London and New York. It represents properties in Europe, Israel, Mexico, and the United States, and its Web site has a special area for Jewish/Kosher rentals.

CyberRentals.com

http://cyberrentals.com

Thousands of rentals in scores of countries and U.S. states are available. Because you make arrangements directly with the owners, prices tend to be competitive.

French Connections

http://www.frenchconnections.co.uk

More than 400 rental accommodations throughout France are listed here.

World Wide Nest

http://www.wwnest.com

Choose from 500-plus listings in France, Greece, Italy, the Canary Islands, Mexico, the Caribbean, California, Florida, and Hawaii.

For more rentals, check Yahoo's links at:

http://dir.yahoo.com/Business_and_Economy/Companies/Travel/Lodging/Vacation_Rentals/

Tip: Compare properties and rates carefully. Some of the higher-end international agencies tack on large commissions, and the same apartment or villa may be available at a lower price from a local agency or the property owner.

CAMPGROUNDS

In the United States and Canada, campgrounds range from basic tent pitches in state forests to Sunbelt RV parks in which "snowbirds" live in $100,000 motorhomes for six months of the year. In Europe, campgrounds often have permanent bungalows for rent. Bottom line: The definition of *campground* varies considerably, and one traveler's campground may be another tourist's holiday resort.

State and local tourist offices usually have information on campgrounds, so check the Web sites in the "Destinations" section. For listings of more campgrounds that you could visit in a lifetime on the road, see:

Camping

http://camping.miningco.com

David Sweet has links to campgrounds, campground directories, camping and RV clubs, national parks and forests, festivals with campgrounds, and just about everything else related to camping in the United States.

Camping Club Europe

http://www.campingclubeurope.com/

This British organization is open to members from abroad, and it provides customized itineraries with campground information. (Click the "Sites" link for sample listings.)

National Park Service

http://www.nps.gov

The U.S. government's PARKNET describes campgrounds in 30 national parks, lakeshores, historic sites, and recreation areas. After you've reviewed the listings, you can make reservations on-line.

HOSTELS

Many hostels (a.k.a. "youth hostels") still have large dormitories, segregated by sex, in which guests sleep in bunk beds and must leave the premises during the day. Other hostels, particularly in Europe, are hard to distinguish from hotels. (My family once stayed at a hostel in the Faroe Islands where our modern, attractive room came with a good-size table and a private bath.)

Hostelling International/American Youth Hostels

http://www.hiayh.org

Hostelling International is the worldwide umbrella organization for more than 4500 hostels in 60-plus countries. Its U.S. affiliate, American Youth Hostels, offers low-cost memberships that give discounts on overnight stays (and, in some cases, priority booking) at hostels around the world. To make reservations, use the International Booking Network.

International Booking Network

http://www.hiayh.org/ushostel/reserva/ibn.htm

With IBN's computerized reservations system, you can phone a domestic number for hostel accommodations in nearly 300 cities and towns in 38 countries.

Hostels of Europe

http://www.hostelseurope.com

This site is famous for its "Top 5 Hostels" list (now expanded to include the Top 10). It lists hostels in most of Europe's major tourist cities, most of which don't require membership in a hostel organization.

Two other good sources of information on hostels and other cheap accommodations are:

Backpacker Network

http://www.thebackpacker.net

These pages may be ugly, but the general backpacking tips are useful. The pages under "countries" list hostels and tourist offices in dozens of countries (including U.S. states and Canadian provinces).

Budget Travel

http://budgettravel.miningco.com

Kelly McCluskey has no shame when it comes to stretching a dollar or drachma, and neither will you after you've spent a few hours exploring his collection of articles and Web links. (When was the last time you saw a Web page entitled "Sleeping in Airports"?)

5
CHAPTER

SPECIAL INTEREST TRAVEL

BUSINESS TRAVEL

Most of the advice in this book applies to business travelers as much as it does to leisure travelers. However, a few Web sites may be especially helpful to corporate road warriors:

Biztravel.com

http://www.biztravel.com

This on-line travel agency has columns and articles for the business traveler. Timesaving freebies include "the world's most advanced mile machine," automated airline upgrades, and paging of your flight status and gate number an hour before departure.

Business Travel

http://businesstravel.miningco.com

Bruce Goldberg delivers hundreds of useful Web links, along with articles such as "Moving Up from Coach" and "Racking Up Miles by Rail."

THEME AND AMUSEMENT PARKS

The term "theme park" may have been invented in the post-Disneyland era, but the concept has been around for hundreds of years. Bakken, in Copenhagen, which claims to be the world's oldest amusement park, dates back to the sixteenth century, and world's fairs and exhibitions have been entertaining the masses since the Victorian Era (if not earlier).

Chances are, there's a theme park or amusement park within commuting distance of your vacation spot. These Web sites can help you check what's available:

Amusement Park and Roller Coaster Links

http://users.sgi.net/~rollocst/amuse.html

This aptly named collection of pages has links to hundreds of parks, rides, observation towers, and related sites.

Theme Parks

http://themeparks.miningco.com

Robert Brown interprets his topic broadly, providing vast numbers of links and scores of articles on theme parks, amusement parks, and zoos around the world. Don't miss the "Ride Physics" links, which will help you understand how engineers harness the forces of nature to leave you trembling after a 60-second ride.

Theme Parks Forum

http://expedia.msn.com/forums/theme/

Microsoft Expedia's Theme Parks Forum has bulletin boards and chat rooms, plus links to host Gary Bungart's "park stats" at www.themeparks.com.

Personal plug: One of my own favorite theme parks is Legoland in Billund, Denmark. A U.S. version recently opened in Carlsbad, California, just north of San Diego (see Figure 5–1). You can visit its Web site at http://www.legolandca.com.

Finally, if you happen to visit Copenhagen between late April and late September, allow at least half a day for:

Tivoli Gardens

http://www.tivoligardens.com

In my article on this downtown theme park at Europe for Visitors, I wrote:

FIGURE 5-1

Legoland, California.

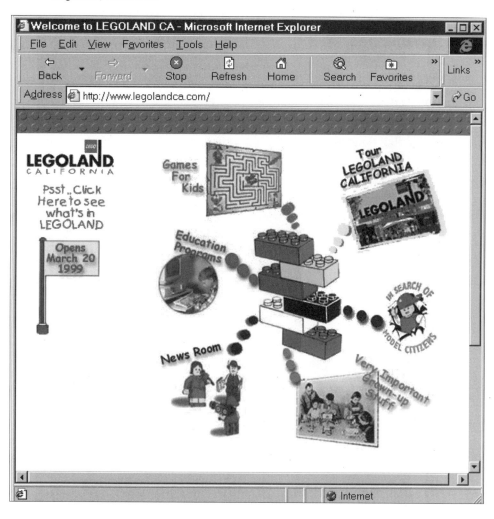

Tivoli's charter required that 75% of the site had to be open space, and that rule—still observed—is one reason why Tivoli feels more like a public garden than a theme park. A buglike roller coaster whirls through the treetops; a Ferris wheel overlooks park benches and flower beds; small motorboats make circles on a scenic lake. While teenagers play games in video arcades, their younger

siblings enjoy a clown show or wave at the costumed king and queen (both children) in the Tivoli Guard parade. Businesspeople wheel and deal over expense account meals, and lovers cuddle on benches as 110,000 bulbs create a romantic glow from dusk until midnight or 1:00 A.M.

ACCESSIBLE TRAVEL

Being saddled with a physical or mental disability doesn't have to mean staying at home. With careful planning, handicapped travelers can enjoy many of the same destinations and experiences as their peers. Here's where to look for on-line travel advice:

Access-Able Travel Source

http://www.access-able.com

Read travel tips, seek advice on a public message board, search an accessible travel database, find a travel agent who specializes in services for disabled travelers, or look up relay and TTY phone numbers for hotel and transportation companies.

Global Access

http://www.geocities.com/Paris/1502/

General advice, Web links, destination features, and a "Readers Write" forum are available at this network for disabled travelers.

For links to Web resources for disabled tourists in the United Kingdom and Western Europe, see my "Accessible Travel" page at:

http://goeurope.miningco.com/msub-accessible.htm

TRAVELING WITH CHILDREN

Hauling the kids along on a trip can be fun, and it doesn't have to mean spending your entire vacation with Minnie Mouse at Disneyland or feeding lambs in a children's zoo. My own children look back fondly on the travel adventures they've had over the years, from wandering through Roman ruins to emergency surgery in an Icelandic fishing port.

The basic rules for traveling with children are:

- **Strike a balance between your wants and theirs.** You want to see the cathedral; they want to visit the playground. Make it clear that (b) is contingent on (a), but also remember that young children don't have unlimited attention spans. (Translation: Skip the 45-minute guided tour and explore at your own pace.)

- **Have a touring base.** If your children know there's a familiar hotel, condo, or cottage waiting at the end of the day, they'll feel less uprooted and edgy while sightseeing.
- **Don't cram too much into your schedule.** Your kids know instinctively that an exhausting pace is no guarantee of a happy vacation. Learn from them.
- **Know when to outsource.** At some point, you'll want to park your kids with a babysitter or entrust them to a resort activity program. Don't feel guilty—just do it, even if it costs you $10 an hour.

Don't take my word for any of this—instead, get advice from an expert at:

Travel with Kids

http://travelwithkids.miningco.com

Teresa Plowright has hauled her children along on Tunisian rug-buying expeditions and traveled in Nepal while pregnant. Her Web site offers tips on everything from family ecotours in Costa Rica to haunted houses and witches' haunts.

GAY/LESBIAN TRAVEL

Gays and lesbians reportedly account for 20 percent of all pleasure travel, so it isn't surprising that an increasing number of resorts and other businesses cater to tourists of the Oscar Wilde or Sapphic persuasion. In a world in which tolerance is never a given, it can be reassuring to stay at hotels or travel with tour groups in which same-sex couples won't be the objects of nasty glances or gossip.

On-line resources for GLBT travelers include:

Gayscene.com

http://www.gayscene.com

Browse 3000-plus listings of gay or gay-friendly hotels, restaurants, clubs, and other businesses on six continents.

PlanetOut Travel

http://www.planetout.com/pno/travel/

Destination guides for the United States, Canada, and Mexico are supplemented by travel articles, a gay/lesbian events calendar, and a directory of gay-friendly travel agents.

PrideNet (Europe)

http://www.pridenet.com/europe.html

Select a country for information on laws, cultural attitudes toward homosexuality, and GLBT business listings.

Rainbow Query: Travel

http://www.rainbowquery.com/Categories/Travel.html

Follow the links to gay travel resources, or enter a keyword search.

ACTIVE/ADVENTURE TRAVEL

Active and adventure travel is a huge topic, ranging from assaults on Mt. Everest to golfing in the Monterey Peninsula. In many cases, you'll find links to helpful information at the Web sites in the "Destinations" section. (Example: Visit any Caribbean Web site, and you'll have to close your eyes to avoid listings for snorkeling and scuba diving.)

For information geared toward travelers who'd rather climb an Alp than ascend a cathedral tower's staircase, see:

Fodor's Sports and Adventure Vacations

http://www.fodors.com/sports

Skydiving, river rafting, caving courses, baseball fantasy camps, fly-fishing schools, race-driving courses, and the inevitable golf camps are a few of the topics covered at this site by Fodor's guidebooks (see Figure 5–2).

GORP

http://www.gorp.com

The Great Outdoor Recreation Pages include sections on biking, hiking, paddling, climbing, camping, and more. Articles and practical information could keep you busy for days (when you should be getting in shape for your trip).

FIGURE 5–2

Fodor's Sports and Adventure Vacations.

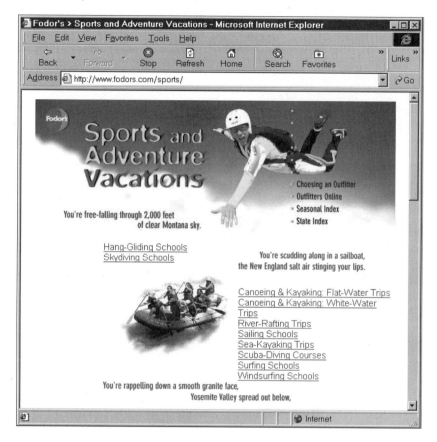

GOLF

Try most URLs in this book's "Destinations" section, and you'll probably find at least one listing for a golf course. I wouldn't be surprised to discover a fairway within chip shot range of the governor's mansion at Colonial Williamsburg.

Still, if you're a serious golfer, you'll find sites that cater to your travel obsession:

GOLFonline

http://www.golfonline.com/travel/

Golf Magazine's Web site has articles on golf travel, plus a database of 18,000 course listings.

Golf-Travel.com

http://www.golf-travel.com

Consult the listings of top U.S. and international resort courses, or read "best" lists for other domestic and foreign courses that are open to the public.

Golf Travel Online

http://gto.com

Use the "Resorts Search" feature to select from 400 golf resorts around the world. Golf tours are also listed.

SKIING/SNOWBOARDING

For information on downhill skiing, cross-country skiing, and snowboarding resorts, try these links:

GoSki

http://www.goski.com

Reports from readers enhance GoSki's evaluations of ski areas in 37 countries.

SkiIN

http://skiin.com

More than 2300 winter resorts in nearly 60 countries are listed, with vital statistics and capsule descriptions of each.

SkiNet.com: Resorts & Travel

http://www.skinet.com/resorts

Browse the 60 top North American ski resorts or search a database of 800 ski areas.

Ski Trips

http://skitrips.miningco.com

Robin Colliander has been writing articles and compiling Web links for winter sports enthusiasts since March of 1997, with topics such as "Chalet Holidays" and "Snow Reports."

ECOTOURISM

The growing popularity of ecotourism creates a dilemma: at what point do visits to unspoiled natural habitats threaten the ecologies that ecotourists want to protect? This is just one of the questions that Ellen Scott confronts at:

Eco-tourism

http://ecotourism.miningco.com

Use this Web site to understand the guiding principles of ecotourism, learn about popular ecotourist destinations, and find ecologically responsible tours and resorts throughout the world.

For more ecotourism listings, visit:

The Green Travel Network

http://www.greentravel.com

Explore "1001 ideas for adventures of a lifetime," using an "Adventure Finder" database of ecologically responsible tour operators.

HONEYMOONS

If you're looking for a resort with heart-shaped bathtubs, tips on getting married on a Caribbean island, or information on special honeymoon travel packages, head for:

Honeymoons

http://honeymoons.miningco.com

Susan Breslow Sardone provides an eclectic blend of honeymoon ideas, from "Honeymoons with Heart" (helping the underprivileged around the world) to "The Romantic's Guide to New York City Museums (with "Gotham's sweetest spots for lovers").

EDUCATIONAL TRAVEL

This is a huge category, and let's face it—any trip can be educational. However, one program for older travelers deserves special mention:

Elderhostel
http://www.elderhostel.org

This not-for-profit organization sponsors archaeology trips to Greece, study cruises in Portugal, dulcimer making in the Appalachians, and other programs in more than 70 countries for travelers from ages 55 and up.

SERVICE TRAVEL

See the world while performing good deeds with:

Global Volunteers
http://www.globalvolunteers.org

Since 1984, more than 6000 travelers have joined Global Volunteers teams for short-term service programs in 20 countries. Many have called their trips "life-changing experiences" and come back for more.

SPAS

Spas range from beauty and weight loss resorts in California to medically supervised European resorts where patients have been "taking the waters" since Roman times.

To find a spa that matches your tastes and needs, immerse yourself in:

Spas
http://spas.miningco.com

Let Julie Register show you where to enjoy mud baths in Bali, aromatherapy in British Columbia, lymph drainage in Baden-Baden, or "specialized body services" in Palm Beach.

6

DESTINATIONS

UNITED STATES

National

Travel America

http://www.travel-america.co.uk

Canadian and British tourists should check the "Travel Advice" section for tips on passports, customs regulations, and medical insurance.

USA Tourist

http://www.usatourist.com

This site is aimed at foreign visitors, but much of the information is useful for Americans exploring their own country.

U.S. National/State Parks

http://usparks.miningco.com

Links to park sites, lists of special events, and articles on national parks and historic sites are a few of the resources at Darren Smith's site. As a bonus, this MiningCo.com guide includes annotated Web links for Canadian parks.

States

Alabama

Alabama Unforgettable
http://www.touralabama.org
The state's official tourism site has listings for every town from
Abbeville to Watumpka.

Alaska

Alaska
http://www.commerce.state.ak.us/tourism/
Use the e-form to request an Alaska Vacation Planner.

Alaska Tourism and Travel Guide
http://www.alaskanet.com/Tourism/
A searchable database lists activities, tours, and places to stay.

Alaska Railroad
http://www.akrr.com
Take the train from the Gulf of Alaska to Anchorage, Denali
National Park, Fairbanks, and beyond.

Arizona

Arizona Guide
http://www.arizonaguide.com
Look up ghost towns, or let the Arizona Office of Tourism suggest
an itinerary based on your interests.

Flagstaff
http://www.flagguide.com
Arizona's four-season mountain city offers a pleasant break from
the desert heat.

Phoenix
http://www.arizonaguide.com/cities/phoenix/
The "golf capital of the world" claims a lower summer Heat Stress
Index than Orlando, Miami, New Orleans, or Dallas.

Best of Tucson

http://www.desert.net/tw/bot/

Use the Arizona Guide for basic tourist info, then come here to find Tucson's leading restaurants, cafés, bars, shops, and entertainment.

Grand Canyon Tourism & National Park Information

http://www.thecanyon.com

What to do, and where to stay, eat, or shop.

Arkansas

Arkansas: The Natural State

http://www.arkansas.com

The Arkansas Department of Parks and Tourism has info on everything from birdwatching to spelunking.

Little Rock

http://www.littlerock.com/lrcvb/

The Arkansas State Capitol is modeled on the U.S. Capitol. Other attractions include the Arkansas Territorial Restoration and Villa Marre, a restored Victorian house with period furnishings.

Hot Springs

http://www.hotsprings.org

Visit Hot Springs National Park, or browse in dozens of antique shops in this historic resort town.

California

California Travel & Tourism

http://gocalif.ca.gov

Use the "Regions" page to select guides for a dozen areas.

San Francisco Guide

http://www.sfguide.com

A simple, fast-loading layout saves time in navigation, but the links in the left column can be hard to read.

San Francisco.com

http://sanfrancisco.com

An alternative guide to the city, featuring the San Francisco *Metropolitan.*

San Francisco for Visitors

http://gosanfran.miningco.com

Tour neighborhoods, pick restaurants, and browse Bay Area travel resources.

Destination LA

http://www.latimes.com/HOME/DESTLA/

The *Los Angeles Times* produces this city guide.

Los Angeles for Visitors

http://gola.miningco.com

The archive of travel articles dates back to 1997, and you'll also find scores of Web links.

San Diego Convention and Visitors Bureau

http://www.sandiego.org

Come for the San Diego Zoo and Sea World, stay for the beaches and benign climate.

Legoland California

http://www.legolandca.com

The plastic-block people have cloned their Danish theme park in a San Diego suburb.

Colorado

Colorado.com

http://www.colorado.com

Drill down from regional maps to city maps, and you'll get a list of attractions.

Colorado for Visitors

http://gocolorado.miningco.com

Links to Colorado tourist offices, ski areas, parks, and accommodations, plus biweekly travel articles.

Colorado Vacation Guide

http://www.coloradoadventure.net

Adventure tours, golf, skiing, scenic drives, and pointers to other Colorado tourism resources.

MileHighCity.com

http://milehighcity.com

A handy directory of things to see and do in Denver.

Connecticut

Connecticut Tourism

http://www.state.ct.us/tourism

Order the free Connecticut Vacation Guide, then head for:

Visit Connecticut

http://www.visitconnecticut.com

Hotels, shopping, and attractions are organized by topic and region. (Click the "VNE" logo for information on other New England states.)

ImBored

http://www.imbored.com/new/index.html

Click any of Connecticut's six regions for a list of things to do when you're bored.

Delaware

Delaware Visitors

http://visitors.delawareonline.com

The News Journal has put together a well-organized guide to the First State.

Scenic South Delaware
http://www.visitdelaware.com

Take a 70-minute ferry ride from New Jersey to Delaware's largest county.

District of Columbia

Washington, D.C. for Visitors
http://godc.miningco.com

Articles and links for the monuments, museums, hotels, restaurants, theatres, transportation, and more.

Florida

Visit Florida
http://www.flausa.com

Tour Florida region by region, clicking links to pages on cities and towns as you go (see Figure 6–1).

Absolutely Florida!
http://www.funandsun.com

Go to the "Florida Beaches" page and click the map for regional directories to public beaches and amenities.

Infoguide Florida
http://www.infoguide.com/

Search a database with 15,000 restaurants and 2600 hotels, or request tee times at 250 golf courses on-line.

Orlando for Visitors
http://goorlando.miningco.com

A guide to Orlando and environs, with links to local theme parks and the Kennedy Space Center.

Miami for Visitors
http://gomiami.miningco.com

A MiningCo.com site on Miami and Miami Beach, with side jaunts to other cities in South Florida.

FIGURE 6–1

Visit Florida (FLA USA).

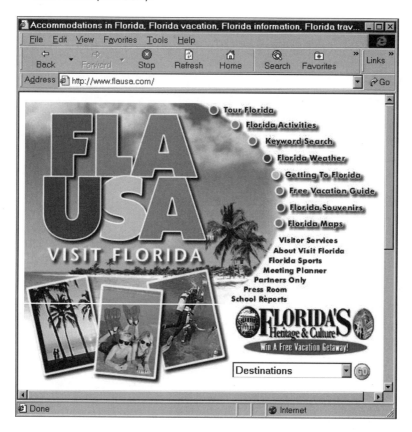

Florida Keys Travel Guide

http://floridakeys.com

Pick a key and click for general information and business listings.

Tampa Bay for Visitors

http://gotampabay.miningco.com

Check the "West Coast Wanderer" page when you're ready to
venture beyond Tampa, St. Petersburg, and Clearwater.

Georgia

Georgia on My Mind

http://www.gomm.com

Click on any of Georgia's nine tourist regions, or scroll down for topics such as "African American Culture" and "Fairs and Festivals."

Insiders' Guide to Atlanta

http://www.insiders.com/atlanta/

When you've finished reading this comprehensive guide, order the print version to tuck in your tote or purse.

Inside Savannah

http://www.insidesavannah.com

Explore this historic city with articles and photographs.

Hawaii

Hawaii

http://www.visit.hawaii.org

The state's official travel site is a good starting point for planning your trip.

Aloha from Hawaii

http://www.aloha-hawaii.com

You'll find a little of everything here, including a "Search Hawaii" database of Hawaiian Web pages.

Hawaii for Visitors

http://gohawaii.miningco.com

Articles and hundreds of Web links to Hawaiian travel resources.

Hawaii: The Big Island

http://www.keycommunications.com/bigisland/

Accommodations, active volcanoes, hiking, and whale watching are a few of the topics covered here.

Idaho

Discover Idaho

http://www.visitid.org

The Idaho Travel and Tourism Guide covers a state with more public lands and wilderness than any other in the Lower 48.

Boise

http://www.boise.org

Ski, ride a stagecoach, or attend the Shakespeare Festival in Idaho's capital.

Sun Valley

http://www.sunvalley.com

When you've had your fill of National Forest campgrounds, enjoy four-star comfort at Idaho's classic resort.

Illinois

Enjoy Illinois!

http://www.enjoyillinois.com

Special sections for African-American and Hispanic visitors add diversity to this state-sponsored site.

Choose Chicago

http://www.chicago.il.org

The Chicago Convention & Visitors Bureau has everything you need to plan your vacation in that toddlin' town.

Virtual El

http://centerstage.net/chicago/virtual-el/

Tour Chicago by subway and "El" train. This guide lists restaurants, theatres, museums, and so forth at each station.

The Web Wanderer's Chicago Guide

http://www.xnet.com/~blatura/chicago.shtml

Find links to weather reports, entertainment guides, museums, and other sites for Chicago visitors.

Galena/Jo Daviess County

http://www.galena.org

Nineteenth-century architecture is beautifully preserved in U. S. Grant's hometown on the Mississippi Bluffs, just three hours west of Chicago (see Figure 6–2).

Indiana

Indiana Tourism

http://www.state.in.us/tourism/

The state's official site is short on info, but you can request literature with the e-form.

Amish Country

http://www.amish-country.com

On your trip through Northern Indiana, stop in Elkhart to borrow the free Heritage Trail Audio Tape Tour.

Indianapolis

http://www.indy.org

Get facts on the Indy 500 and more.

Iowa

Iowa

http://www.icvba.org

Click a name on the map for local tourist information.

Des Moines

http://www.desmoinesia.com

What to see, where to sleep, and how to dine in a city once known as Fort Raccoon.

Amana Colonies

http://www.jeonet.com/amanas/

Visit historic sites in the seven Amana villages, then shop for furniture, woolens, and other traditional products.

FIGURE 6–2

Galena/Jo Daviess County.

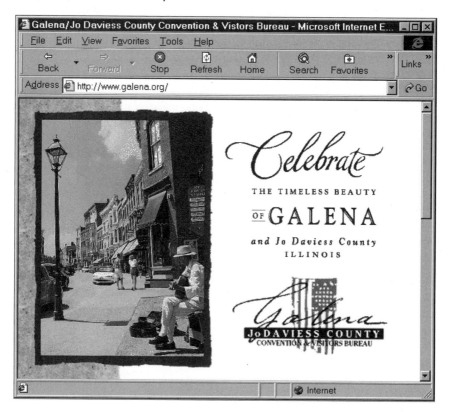

Kansas

Kansas: Simply Wonderful
http://www.kansascommerce.com/0400travel.html
Plan a vacation on-line, or check the calendar of events in America's middlemost state.

Kansas Sights
http://raven.cc.ukans.edu/heritage/kssights/
Nancy Sween's travel site includes a sing-along chorus of "Home on the Range."

Experience Kansas City

http://www.experiencekc.com

There are actually *two* Kansas Cities: a little one in Kansas, and a bigger one in Missouri.

Lawrence

http://www.visitlawrence.com

The University of Kansas and Haskell Indian Nations University make this a lively college town.

Kentucky

Official Kentucky Vacation Guide

http://www.kentuckytourism.com

The Bluegrass State has a great tourism site with pages for scores of cities and towns.

Kentucky Tourism Council

http://www.tourky.com

You'll find all the basics here: sights, hotels, festivals, and more.

Online Guide to Greater Louisville

http://www.louisville-visitors.com

Churchill Downs, site of the Kentucky Derby, is merely the most famous of Louisville's attractions.

Insider's Guide to Greater Lexington

http://www.insiders.com/lexington-ky/

Sip bourbon, watch the races, and enjoy a smoke.

Louisiana

Louisiana

http://www.crt.state.la.us/crt/tourism.htm

This site divides Louisiana into five regions and offers tourist information for each.

Louisiana Travel

http://www.louisianatravel.com

Use the database to find hotels, B&Bs, campgrounds, festivals, golf, gardens, and a lot more.

New Orleans Online

http://neworleansonline.com

The lodgings and restaurant database is handy; the history and attractions pages are equally useful.

Best of New Orleans

http://www.bestofneworleans.com

Gambit Weekly, a local magazine, lists "everything worth knowing, doing, and seeing in the Big Easy."

Cajun Life

http://www.cajunlife.com

South Louisiana claims the nickname "Little France."

Maine

Welcome to Maine

http://www.visitmaine.com

Spend hours (or days) touring Maine before your trip.

Explore Maine

http://maineguide.com/region/

Select a region or town, then click "go" for local business listings (some with links).

Maine's Coast

http://www.geocities.com/Yosemite/1465/

Ignore the annoying GeoCities pop-up ads as you tour coastal Maine in text and pictures.

Lobster.net

http://www.chickadee.com/lobster/

Four towns along the Southern Maine Seacoast are known for catching lobsters—and visitors.

Maryland

Maryland

http://www.mdisfun.org

"So many things to do, so close together" is an apt tourism motto for the Free State.

Annapolis & Anne Arundel County

http://visit-annapolis.org

"America's sailing capital" is also home to the U.S. Naval Academy.

Beach-Net!

http://www.beach-net.com

Ocean City and other coastal communities are featured here, along with road directions from nine states.

Tilghman Island

http://www.tilghmanisland.com

Vacation in the middle of Chesapeake Bay.

Massachusetts

Massachusetts

http://www.mass-vacation.com

Pick a destination, plan a trip, check winter ski reports.

Boston USA

http://www.bostonusa.com

The Greater Boston Convention & Visitors Bureau describes more than 1000 "points of interest" and other items for visitors.

Underground Guide to Boston

http://www.newbury.com/guide.htm

Learn about neighborhoods, body-piercing parlors, and veggie-friendly restaurants.

Berkshire Visitors Bureau

http://www.berkshires.org

"America's premier cultural resort" is pretty and easy to reach from Boston or New York.

Cape Cod

http://www.capecodchamber.org

Play golf, go fishing, watch the whales, or have a wedding.

Martha's Vineyard

http://www.mvy.com

Ferry schedules, cottage rentals, and bike paths are a few of the topics on the island's Web site.

Nantucket Island

http://www.allcapecod.com/nantucket/

"The Timeless Island" is 30 miles off the Massachusetts coast.

Michigan

Travel Michigan

http://www.michigan.org

Don't head for either peninsula until you've explored the Travel Planner database.

Detroit

http://www.visitdetroit.com

Click the "Visitor's Guides" link to order a free information kit.

The Fabulous Ruins of Detroit

http://www.bhere.com/ruins/

A photographic tour of Detroit's greatest landmarks—some vanished, some still visible to tourists.

Northern Michigan Connection

http://www.michiweb.com

When you're ready to get away from it all, head for the U.P.

Shepler's Mackinac Island Ferries

http://www.sheplerswww.com

Take the boat to the Midwest's most famous resort island.

Minnesota

Explore Minnesota
http://www.exploreminnesota.com
Come for the fishing in 10,000 lakes, stay to shop in America's largest mall.

@Minneapolis
http://www.minneapolis.org
The Greater Minneapolis Convention & Visitors Association dispenses advice on hotels, sightseeing, accommodations, and Indian casinos.

Downtown Minneapolis
http://www.downtownmpls.com
Enjoy major-league sports, shopping, music, theater, and Holidazzle Parades beneath the "skyways."

Uptown on the Web
http://www.writing.org/uptown.htm
The Greenwich Village of the Upper Midwest hosts one of the country's largest art fairs during August.

Saint Paul CityGuide
http://www.saint-paul.com
Minnesota's capital has downtown museums and an annual Winter Carnival.

Duluth
http://www.cp.duluth.mn.us/~team/
The largest city on Lake Superior is a tourist's delight, especially in summer.

Mississippi

Mississippi
http://www.decd.state.ms.us/tourism.htm
"The South's warmest welcome" may not be an appealing motto during August, but don't miss Natchez and other historic towns during spring and fall.

Mississippi Gulf Coast

http://www.gulfcoast.org/mgccvb/

Attractions here include resorts like Biloxi and the Gulf Islands National Seashore.

Missouri

Missouri

http://www.missouritourism.org

"Where the rivers run" is the new marketing theme of Harry Truman's home state.

Show Me Missouri

http://www.show-me-missouri.com

Use the interactive map to explore Missouri's 10 regions.

St. Louis

http://www.st-louis-cvc.com

Use the Visitor's Guide for advice on lodgings, dining, sightseeing, and local transportation.

Kansas City, MO

http://kansascity.miningco.com

When you've finished exploring the articles and links on this site, check "Experience Kansas City" under my listings for Kansas.

Montana

Montana: Big Sky Country

http://travel.mt.gov

Explore 8000 listings of attractions, lodgings, and other tourist businesses in this state of cowboys, copper miners, and movie stars.

Montana's Winter Recreation Opportunities

http://www.wintermt.com

Ski, snowboard, roar across Montana in a snowmobile, or even mush a sled dog team.

Grand Teton Lodge Company

http://www.gtlc.com

Sleep and dine in style during your visit to Grand Teton National Park.

Nebraska

Nebraska

http://www.visitnebraska.org

Plan a trip here, or use the Electronic Travel Information System terminals in kiosks at rest areas and other locations.

Welcome to Omaha

http://www.visitomaha.com

The Mormon Trail Center at Winter Quarters, the Gerald R. Ford Birthplace, and the Henry Doorly Zoo prove that Omaha has more to offer than beef.

Lincoln

http://www.lincoln.org/cvb/

Visit the governor's mansion, the roller skating museum, and the 14th-floor observation deck of the State Capitol.

Nevada

Nevada

http://www.travelnevada.com

Go to the chapel, go skiing, go broke at the casinos, or go to America's newest National Parks.

The Nevada Gambler

http://www.elguru.com

Even if your idea of gaming is an evening of Monopoly, you'll find useful tourist information here.

Las Vegas

http://www.lasvegas24hours.com

More than 30 million people arrive in Las Vegas every year. You can avoid many of them by visiting between Monday and Thursday.

Hoover Dam

http://www.hooverdam.com

Tour the "Virtual Visitors Center" to see how a hydroelectric generating plant works.

Reno/Lake Tahoe

http://www.playreno.com

There was a time when divorce was Reno's biggest industry; today, the big attractions are golf, gambling, and skiing or boating at nearby Lake Tahoe.

New Hampshire

New Hampshire

http://www.visitnh.gov

Order a free guidebook of 200-plus pages, or explore the state's seven regions on-line.

Visit New Hampshire

http://www.visit-newhampshire.com

This well-organized commercial site makes it easy to find accommodations, local tourist offices, and other information.

White Mountain Attractions

http://www.whitemtn.org

View a slide show, or get details on what to see and do amid New Hampshire's most famous scenery.

ImBored: New Hampshire

http://www.imbored.com/new/rnh01.htm

What to do (and where to do it) when you can't think of anything to do.

New Jersey

New Jersey Attractions

http://www.go-newjersey.com

Click a category, such as "museums" or "events," to see listings by city or town.

Virtual New Jersey Shore

http://www.virtualnjshore.com

This site lists beaches, parks, and resort towns along New Jersey's Atlantic coastline, from Keansburg to Cape May.

Atlantic City Nights

http://www.acnights.com

A guide to casinos, restaurants, nightclubs, and other nighttime activities, plus a hotel search engine.

New Mexico

New Mexico: Land of Enchantment

http://www.newmexico.org

Hispanic and Indian culture are New Mexico's major draws, with outdoor activities not far behind.

New Mexico for Visitors

http://gonewmexico.miningco.com

Boise Matthews offers dozens of travel articles and hundreds of links at her MiningCo.com site.

New Mexico's Cultural Treasures

http://www.nmculture.org

New Mexico's museums, parks, and monuments are covered in depth, with information on fees and opening hours.

Albuquerque

http://www.abqcvb.org

Use the "self-guided tours" page to map out your stay in New Mexico's largest city.

Santa Fe

http://www.santafe.org

The sleepy Hispanic town of yesteryear is now a mecca for tourists, artists, and opera fans.

Carlsbad Caverns

http://www.nps.gov/cave/

The world's largest limestone cavern is one of the 83 separate caves at Carlsbad.

New York

New York State

http://iloveny.state.ny.us

Tour the Empire State's regions, request literature, or even apply for an official "I Love NY" MasterCard.

Upstate New York

http://www.roundthebend.com

The Adirondacks, Catskills, Finger Lakes, and Thousand Islands are among the 10 regions covered here.

Western New York Travel Guide

http://www.westernny.com

The Chautauqua Institution and Niagara Falls are two of this area's popular attractions.

New York Canals

http://www.canals.state.ny.us

Enjoy a sightseeing excursion, an overnight cruise, or a boat rental on 524 miles of historic waterways.

New York City!

http://www.nycvisit.com

The city's official tourism site is packed with useful info, such as a "Big Apple Bargains" page of attractions that are free or under $10.

New York City for Visitors

http://gonyc.miningco.com

Julie Altebrando's father was a catering manager at the Plaza and the Waldorf; she follows the family tradition by serving a tempting menu of articles and links.

NYCTourist.com

http://www.nyctourist.com

Photo tours of famous sights, hotels, restaurants, shopping, sightseeing tours, Broadway shows, and Top 10 lists are featured on this commercial site.

New York City Transportation Maps

http://www.ci.nyc.ny.us/html/dot/html/transportation_maps/home.html

Bike routes, borough maps, transit information, and lists of taxi stands are just a mouseclick away.

Toilets.nyc

http://www.itp.tsoa.nyu.edu/~student/elecpub/kain/

"Where do you want to go today?" isn't just a Microsoft slogan; it's also the motto of this restroom locator in New York City (see Figure 6–3).

North Carolina

North Carolina

http://www.visitnc.com

Head for the heartland, the mountains, or the coast, then choose a town for local information.

Visit North Carolina Destinations

http://visit.nc.org

Reach the official tourism sites for nearly 30 cities by using the links in the drop-down list.

Smoky Search

http://smokysearch.com

The links here point to Smoky Mountain attractions in North Carolina and Tennessee.

NCDOT Ferry Connection

http://www.dot.state.nc.us/transit/ferry/

More than 2.5 million passengers and 900,000 vehicles reach the Outer Banks and other coastal areas by ferry each year.

FIGURE 6–3

Toilets.nyc.

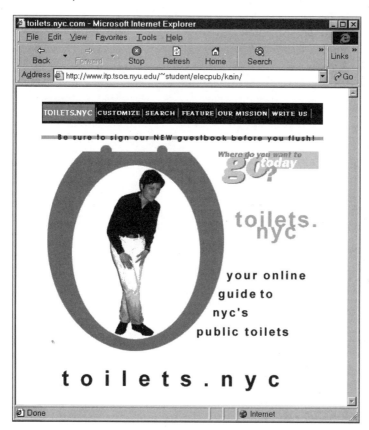

North Dakota

DIRT!

http://www.kt-web.com/nddirt/

Kirk Samuelson wrote this "Down to Earth Guide to North Dakota."

North Dakota's Most Famous Cities

http://www.kt-web.com/nddirt/cit/cit.html

Visit Antwerp, Dresden, Lisbon, Sydney, and Havana, or 13 other famous cities without leaving North Dakota.

Ohio

Ohio

http://www.ohiotourism.com

Drill down through the index, or use the search form to locate information on everything from "Amish" to "Wineries."

Travel Ohio Internet Guide

http://www.travelohio.com

This frequently updated site features events and attractions in 10 regions.

Insider's Guide to Greater Cincinnati

http://www.insiders.com/cincinnati/

Local authors wrote this guide, which is also available as a book.

Greater Cleveland Visitors Guide

http://www.cleve-visitors-guide.com

The Pro Football and Rock & Roll Halls of Fame are two of the Cleveland area's popular attractions.

Oklahoma

Oklahoma Native America

http://www.travelok.com

In addition to a trip planner, this state-sponsored site has a game, an on-line movie, and a student guide.

Oklahoma City Visitors' Center

http://www.okccvb.org

Attend the Red Earth Festival, and visit the National Cowboy Hall of Fame.

Bret's Slightly Warped Tour of Tulsa

http://www.ionet.net/%7ebretp/

Take a photo tour of Tulsa, with commentary and links to places of interest (such as the 60-foot praying hands at Oral Roberts University, said to be the largest bronze casting in the world).

Tulsa Area Museums

http://tulsaweb.com/MUSEUM.HTM

The Will Rogers Memorial & Birthplace and the Tulsa Air & Space Center are among the 14 attractions listed here.

Oregon

Oregon

http://www.traveloregon.com

Explore dunes and lighthouses, cattle and sheep ranches, wild rivers and mountain ridges.

Oregon Coast Travel Guide

http://www.teleport.com/~coastal/

Click on "coastal maps" to plan a trip along Oregon's Pacific seashore.

Oregon Coast Alterna-Guide

http://www.navicom.com/~andrehage/alternacoast.html

Learn about dunes that sing, glowing sand, and "romantic spots secluded enough for naughtiness."

Portland Visitor Information

http://www.pova.com/visitor/index.html

Portland is one of America's most livable cities, and it isn't a bad place to visit, either.

Portland Low-Budget Guide

http://www.hevanet.com/chezxx/low-rent/

Explore the City of Roses for the price of a daisy bouquet.

Pennsylvania

Pennsylvania

http://www.state.pa.us/visit/index1.html

The Commonwealth, a.k.a. the Keystone State, offers a wealth of uncommon sights and scenery.

Pennsylvania Dutch Country

http://www.800padutch.com

The Amish lifestyle is alive and well in Lancaster County.

Philadelphia

http://www.libertynet.org/phila-visitor/

After you've seen Independence Hall and the Liberty Bell, tour the Eastern State Penitentiary.

Greater Pittsburgh

http://www.pittsburgh-cvb.org

This site is rather skimpy; for accommodations info, see:

Pittsburgh Bed & Breakfast Association

http://www.pittsburghbnb.com

More than a dozen B&Bs are listed for the city and environs, with photos and descriptions of each.

Gettysburg Address

http://www.gettysburgaddress.com

If you can't wait to see the Civil War battlefield, get an advance peek with the Webcam on Gettysburg's 393-foot viewing tower.

Rhode Island

Visit Rhode Island

http://www.visitrhodeisland.com

Seven tourism regions are squeezed into America's smallest state.

Visit RI

http://www.visitri.com

Another state guide, this one unofficial.

Newport

http://www.gonewport.com

"America's first resort" is famous for yachting, mansions, and its yearly Jazz Festival.

Providence

http://www.providencecvb.com

See Waterfire, explore Little Italy, tour the State House, and visit the Battleship Massachusetts in nearby Fall River.

Discover the Coastal Villages

http://www.coastalvillages.com

Three villages in Rhode Island and three in Massachusetts offer a taste of traditional life along New England's shores and inlets.

South Carolina

South Carolina

http://www.sccsi.com/sc/

"Smiling Faces, Beautiful Places" is the state's trademarked tourist theme.

Charleston Online Visitors Guide

http://www.charlestoncvb.com

Condé Nast Traveler magazine has named "The Holy City" a Top 10 vacation destination for six years in a row.

The Ghosts of Charleston Tour

http://www.tourcharleston.com

Don't see the ghosts without a guide (see Figure 6–4).

Hilton Head Island Welcome Center

http://hiltonheadisland.net

When you've had your fill of beaches, nature preserves, and golf, head for the many outlet stores.

Myrtle Beach Live

http://www.myrtlebeachlive.com

Build a sandcastle, fish for 29 species, or choose from 89 golf courses in or near Myrtle Beach.

FIGURE 6–4

The Ghosts of Charleston Tour.

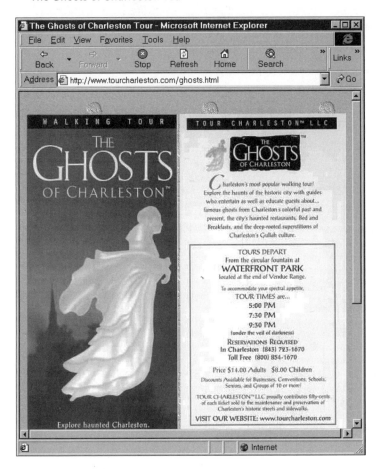

Explore haunted Charleston.

South Dakota

South Dakota

http://www.state.sd.us./state/executive/tourism/

Sure, you've got to visit Mount Rushmore and the Badlands—but not before you've seen the Corn Palace in Mitchell.

Rapid City: Star of the West

http://www.rapidcitycvb.com

Rapid City is the gateway to the Black Hills; fill your gas tank before you leave town.

Deadwood

http://www.deadwood.net

The Wild West meets Casino Country in a town famous for Wild Bill Hickok, Wyatt Earp, and Calamity Jane.

Explore Dickinson

http://www.dickinsoncvb.com

Come for the Roughrider Days; stay for the Ukrainian Festival, Dinosaur Museum, and Assumption Abbey.

Tennessee

Tennessee

http://www.tourism.state.tn.us

Take an on-line tour or request a free vacation planner.

Rod's Guide to the Smoky Mountains

http://www.rodsguide.com

Hiking, fishing, crafts, events, cabin rentals, and weddings are some of the topics covered here.

Tennessee's Backroads

http://www.tennweb.com/tnbkrds/

Visit the home of Tennessee sour mash whiskey and the Tennessee walking horse.

Chattanooga

http://www.chattanooga.net/cvb/

The Tennessee Aquarium, Civil War Museum, and riverboat *Southern Belle* are a few of Chattanooga's attractions.

Memphis

http://www.memphistravel.com

"When other cities show off their skylines, we show off our sounds," says the home of the blues and the birthplace of rock 'n' roll.

Nashville

http://www.nashvillecvb.com

If you're into the twang thang, don't miss the Grand Ole Opry and the Country Music Hall of Fame. Andrew Jackson's home is worth visiting, too.

Texas

TravelTex

http://traveltex.com

"It's like a whole other country," and you'll find plenty of places to visit on the official state tourism site's interactive map.

The East Texas Guide

http://www.easttexasguide.com

Dallas and Houston are the biggest cities in this region; other familiar names include Carthage, Paris, and Palestine.

The Gulf Coast & South Texas

http://pw2.netcom.com/~wandaron/cotxroads.html

This site has information and links for Galveston, Beaumont, Houston, and other areas near the coast.

Austin

http://www.austin360.com/acvb

See the State Capitol, enjoy live music, explore the Texas Hill Country, or watch a million bats take flight at dusk.

Dallas

http://www.dallascvb.com

Big business, big culture, and big skyscrapers make Dallas feel like a Texas version of Chicago.

Fort Worth

http://www.fortworth.com

"Don't take whoa for an answer," say the residents of Dallas's sister city, which takes pride in its Western heritage.

Houston

http://www.houston-guide.com

The Space Center is a big draw; so are Six Flags AstroWorld and the new Bayou Place entertainment complex.

San Antonio

http://www.sanantoniocvb.com

Tour the Alamo and the Spanish Governor's Palace, stroll along the River Walk, shop for arts and crafts in La Villita.

Utah

Utah!

http://www.utah.com

Get general tourist information from the Utah Travel Council, or click to the secondary sites for skiing, rafting, bicycling, and golf.

Utah for Visitors

http://goutah.miningco.com

Theresa Husarik, a wildlife and nature photographer in Salt Lake City, updates her site regularly with new travel articles and Web links.

Visit Salt Lake City

http://www.visitsaltlakecity.com

The Great Salt Lake and world-class ski resorts are within a short ride of Temple Square.

Moab

http://moab-utah.com

Arches and Canyonlands National Parks draw visitors to Moab, in Utah's arid and rugged southeastern corner.

Sundance

http://www.infowest.com/Utah/

Skiing is just one aspect of Robert Redford's mountain community, which has cultural events and art activities year-round.

Vermont

Vermont Traveler's Guide

http://www.travel-vermont.com

The Green Mountains, covered bridges, picturesque villages, and classic East Coast skiing are Vermont's big attractions.

Discover Vermont

http://www.discover-vermont.com

Use the database search forms to find lodgings, restaurants, events, and more.

Vermont Guides

http://www.vtguides.com

This site displays a winter or summer guide, depending on the time of year.

ImBored: Vermont

http://www.imbored.com/new/rvt01.htm

Where to bowl, golf, swim, buy antiques, eat ice cream, and so forth in Vermont.

Lake Champlain Ferries

http://www.ferries.com

Cross the lake to New York State and the Adirondacks from Grand Isle, Burlington, or Charlotte.

Virginia

Visit Virginia

http://www.virginia.org

"Virginia is for lovers" celebrates its 30th year as the tourist motto of a state that gave birth to George Washington and Thomas Jefferson.

The Virginia Waterfront

http://www.thevirginiawaterfront.com

Tour Virginia's coastal cities, from Williamsburg to Virginia Beach.

Richmond

http://www.richmondva.org

The capital of the Confederacy produced the world's first canned beer in 1935.

Colonial Williamsburg

http://www.history.org

See history brought to life—and if you can afford it, stay overnight in a colonial house or official hotel (see Figure 6–5).

FIGURE 6–5

Colonial Williamsburg.

Historic Mount Vernon

http://www.mountvernon.org

George Washington slept here—and still does.

Washington

Washington State

http://www.tourism.wa.gov

The state's official tourism site is a bit skimpy, so don't miss:

Travel in Washington

http://www.travel-in-wa.com

Fast-loading text pages make it easy to find the details you need, but you'll also find a photo gallery and QuickTime "virtual visits" for leisurely on-line touring.

Olympic Peninsula Travel Association

http://www.waypt.com/opta/

Take the ferry from Seattle, Victoria, or other points, then tour the peninsula via the recommended scenic loops.

Seattle-King County

http://www.seeseattle.org/home/skccvb.htm

Skip the suburbs and stay downtown. Don't miss the city's best sightseeing bargain: a ride on the Bainbridge Island ferry.

Mosquito Fleet

http://www.whalewatching.com

Spy on orcas or catch a passenger ferry to the San Juans.

San Juan Islands Guide

http://www.sanjuanguide.com

This island group is popular with sailors, anglers, hikers, bikers, and summer people.

Spokane.org

http://www.spokane.org

Click "Convention & Visitors" bureau for travel information on Washington's biggest city east of the Cascades.

West Virginia

West Virginia: Wild and Wonderful

http://www.state.wv.us/tourism/

Outdoor recreation is popular in West Virginia; so are tours of the state's glass studios, factories, and museums.

West Virginia: It's You

http://www.westvirginia.com

Eight regions are covered, from Mountain Lakes to the Mid-Ohio Valley.

Harper's Ferry National Historical Park

http://www.nps.gov/hafe/home.htm

John Brown's attempt to free slaves here in 1859 pushed the United States toward Civil War.

Wisconsin

Wisconsin

http://tourism.state.wi.us

Fish in the North Woods, enjoy family fun in the Wisconsin Dells, or tour breweries and ride Lake Michigan excursion boats in Milwaukee.

Tour Wisconsin

http://www.innsite.com/wbba/wisc.html

The Wisconsin Bed & Breakfast Association offers detailed motoring itineraries, with links to B&Bs in each region.

Greater Milwaukee

http://www.milwaukee.org/visit.htm

Wisconsin's largest city is famous for beer and baseball; other attractions include Summerfest and ethnic events throughout the year.

Greater Madison

http://www.visitmadison.com

The state capital is also home to the University of Wisconsin's lakefront campus.

Wisconsin Dells

http://www.dells.com

The emphasis here is on family fun, and the most popular souvenir is a bumper sticker from Tommy Bartlett's Thrill Show.

Wyoming

Wyoming

http://www.state.wy.us/state/tourism/tourism.html

This site's interface is reminiscent of the Web circa 1994, but it does provide useful information.

Wyoming Electronic Scout

http://commerce.state.wy.us/west/recreation/

Click "Planning your trip" for advice on places to visit, places to stay, and things to do.

Cheyenne

http://www.cheyenne.org

Wyoming's state capital plays up its Western heritage with Frontier Days, "gunslinger gunfights," and rodeos three nights a week during summer.

Mountain Country Visitor's Guide

http://www.jacksonholenet.com/mountainctry/

Jackson Hole and Wyoming's National Parks are the focus of these pages for family and adventure travelers.

CANADA

National

Travel Canada

http://www.canadatourism.com/ctc/travel_canada/

This government site is a great starting place for planning your Canadian vacation.

Canada for Visitors

http://gocanada.miningco.com

Elke Mairs offers a massive library of Web links and articles for travelers to Canada.

Provinces/Territories

Alberta

Discover Alberta

http://www.discoveralberta.com

You'll find everything here—even a wedding planner!

Calgary

http://www.discovercalgary.com

Rustling is frowned upon, but there's plenty of cattle rassling at the annual Stampede.

Edmonton

http://www.discoveredmonton.com

When the cold winter comes, take shelter in the world's largest shopping mall.

Banff-Lake Louise

http://www.banfflakelouise.com

Tour the National Park, ride the Sulphur Mountain Gondola, or come for skiing in the winter.

Jasper

http://www.discoverjasper.com

Jasper National Park, Canada's longest aerial tramway, and rides on the Columbia Icefields are things to enjoy in Jasper.

British Columbia

British Columbia Adventure Network

http://bcadventure.com/adventure/

Among its other top-notch features, this privately operated site has some of the best local maps you'll find on-line.

Tourism Vancouver

http://www.tourism-vancouver.org

The city's official tourism Web has all the usual amenities.

Destination: Vancouver

http://www.netminder.com/yvr/

You've got to admire a tourist pitch that begins with the statement, "It often rains in Vancouver."

Victoria & Vancouver Island, Gulf Islands

http://victoriabc.com

Some come for high tea at the Empress Hotel, others for lovely gardens, and a few for the 140-foot bungee jump.

WhistlerWEB.net

http://www.whistlerweb.net

If Whistler's world-class skiing and snowboarding aren't your fancy, come in summer for kayaking, rafting, trout fishing, and golf.

Lighthouses of British Columbia

http://aspen.bc.ca/bclights/

When you're cruising along the coast, keep an eye on these lights.

Manitoba

Explore Manitoba

http://www.travelmanitoba.com

One hundred thousand lakes are just one reason to visit Manitoba—but if you're adventurous, head north to Hudson Bay.

Manitoba Fishing and Outdoors Information

http://www.winnipeg.freenet.mb.ca/mfo/

Northerns and walleye are Manitoba's big draws for visiting anglers.

Winnipeg

http://www.tourism.winnipeg.mb.ca

Six hundred fifty thousand people live in the capital of "Canada's most ethnically diverse province."

New Brunswick

New Brunswick

http://www.cybersmith.net/nbtour/

This bilingual Atlantic province claims the warmest saltwater beaches north of Virginia.

Saint John

http://www.city.saint-john.nb.ca

Canada's oldest city is on the Bay of Fundy. Its famous "reversing waterfalls" change direction with the world's highest tides.

Quoddy Loop Tour Guide

http://www.quoddyloop.com

Take a "two-nation vacation" on the Bay of Fundy.

Newfoundland

Newfoundland & Labrador

http://www.gov.nf.ca/tourism/

The easternmost area of North America was settled by Vikings 1000 years ago.

Welcome to Labrador

http://www.geocities.com/Yosemite/Rapids/3330/

Take a boat up the North Coast or head inland on the Trans-Labrador Highway.

St. John's

http://www.city.st-johns.nf.ca

The Signal Hill Tattoo, whale watching, and iceberg viewing are popular activities in this provincial capital and fishing port.

Northwest Territories

NWT Explorer's Guide

http://www.nwttravel.nt.ca

If Alaska and the Yukon seem too crowded, pitch your tent in the Northwest Territories.

Canada's Arctic Area Guide

http://www.areaguide.net/arctic/

In addition to basic tourist info, you'll find links to Yellowknife and Baffin Island pages here.

Nova Scotia

Virtual Nova Scotia

http://explore.gov.ns.ca

Nova Scotia is nicknamed "Canada's ocean playground," so it's appropriate—and fun—to arrive by ferry.

Destination: Nova Scotia

http://www.destination-ns.com

Order a free travel guide, then learn about driving itineraries, music, and golf.

Halifax Visitor Information

http://www.halifaxinfo.com

Some 150 *Titanic* victims are buried in Halifax, and the city's Maritime Museum has a permanent exhibit of artifacts from the ship.

Cape Breton Island

http://www.cbisland.com

Attractions on Cape Breton include the Fortress of Louisbourg, a living-history museum that's said to be the largest historic restoration in North America.

Nunavut

Nunavut Tourism

http://www.nunatour.nt.ca

Nunavut, an Arctic region of 18,000 Inuit people, became a self-governing territory in April 1999.

Ontario

Ontario

http://204.101.2.101/travel/

The Ontario government's site covers most of the basics, from "aboriginal-owned lodges and cabins" to water transportation.

Travelinx Ontario

http://www.travelinx.com

If you know what to ask, this collection of database query forms will help you zero in on places to stay and things to do.

Ottawa

http://www.tourottawa.org

Visit Parliament Hill, tour national museums, see the RCMP stables, or skate with the commuters on a frozen canal.

Tourism Toronto

http://www.tourism-toronto.com

The UN has named Toronto "the world's most ethnically diverse city," and you can see it all from the world's tallest building.

Toronto City Guide

http://www.rickym.com/cityguide/

Tell 'em you saw it on Ricky McMountain.

Toronto Transit Commission

http://www.city.toronto.on.ca/ttc

Why drive when you can take the subway, streetcar, or bus?

Prince Edward Island

Prince Edward Island

http://www.gov.pe.ca/vg/index.asp

Jacques Cartier landed on PEI in 1534; three centuries later, Charlottetown became Canada's birthplace.

Cavendish

http://town.cavendish.pe.ca

The novel *Anne of Green Gables* was inspired by Green Cables farm, which you can visit in PEI National Park.

Charlottetown Festival

http://www.confederationcentre.com

Anne of Green Gables: The Musical is just one of the traditional summer events in Charlottetown, the "birthplace of Canada."

Quebec

Tourisme Québec

http://www.tourisme.gouv.qc.ca

Click "English Version" if *vous ne parlez pas français.*

Québec Tourist Guide

http://www.quebecweb.com/tourisme/introang.html

This site's design is a bit rustic, but the information is useful and the photos are appealing.

Destination Québec

http://www.destinationquebec.com

Select "English," then search for lodgings, restaurants, activities, festivals, culture, and more.

Montréal

http://www.tourism-montreal.org

The world's largest French-speaking city outside Paris presents a world-class Expo of tourist information.

Quebec City—Ville de Québec

http://www.quebec-region.cuq.qc.ca

If you can't spend your honeymoon within the walls of romantic Quebec City, come for the Winter Carnival (see Figure 6–6).

Tremblant

http://www.tremblant.ca/e/winter/

Quebec's highest ski mountain claims the largest terrain in Eastern North America.

Saskatchewan

Saskatchewan

http://www.sasktourism.com

The Royal Canadian Mounted Police are headquartered in Saskatchewan. Other attractions include fossils, Indian culture, and some 250 museums.

FIGURE 6-6

Quebec City—Ville de Québec.

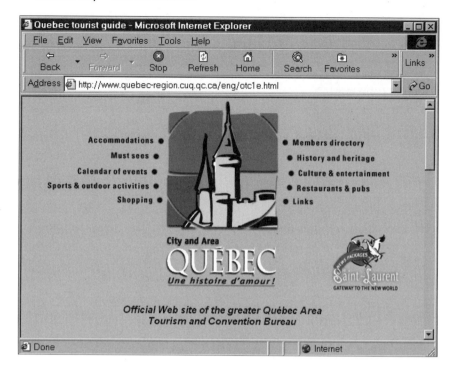

Regina

http://www.tourismregina.com

Tour the capital's Legislative Building, visit the RCMP Museum, attend a festival, or go for broke in the Casino.

Yukon

Tour Yukon

http://www.touryukon.com

Bring a dogsled, leave your tuxedo at home, and be prepared to rassle with trout the size of a tuna.

Klondike Visitors Association

http://www.hyperborean-web.com/kva/

Pan for gold at Free Claim No. 6, or pay homage to the Klondike's most famous author at the Jack London Interpretive Center.

Whitehorse
http://www.city.whitehorse.yk.ca
The Yukon's capital has a paddlewheel steamer, museums, and a surprising number of major events throughout the year.

CARIBBEAN
General Information

Caribbean.com
http://www.caribbean.com
This site offers one-page introductions to 29 Caribbean islands and countries.

Caribbean-on-line
http://caribbean-on-line.com
Click an island on the map for local tourist information.

Anguilla

Anguilla
http://www.candw.com.ai/~atbtour/
The "wreck dive capital of the Caribbean" lies 150 miles east of Puerto Rico, in the Leeward Islands.

Antigua and Barbuda

Antigua & Barbuda
http://www.interknowledge.com/antigua-barbuda/
Lord Nelson established a naval base here in 1784; today, men-of-war have been replaced by racing yachts, dive boats, and beach blankets.

Aruba

Aruba
http://www.aruba.com
The northern coast's cliffs and grottoes give way to a desert interior, whereas Aruba's south and west coasts are lined with white-sand beaches.

Bahamas

The Islands of The Bahamas

http://bahamas.com

Eleuthera, Grand Bahama, and Nassau are merely the best known of the 700 islands and cays in this British Commonwealth nation.

Barbados

Barbados Tourism Encyclopedia

http://www.barbados.org

This flat island is made largely of coral, and it offers activities that range from cricket to golf to windsurfing.

Bermuda

Bermuda

http://www.bermudatourism.org

Old British forts, the sixteenth- and seventeenth-century town of St. George, nature preserves, and caves vie with outdoor activities for the tourist's attention in Bermuda.

Bonaire

Bonaire Dutch Caribbean

http://www.interknowledge.com/bonaire/

Bonaire, in the Dutch Antilles, offers something for everyone—from scuba divers and beach bums to wildlife buffs.

British Virgin Islands

British Virgin Islands Home Page

http://www.britishvirginislands.com

This commercial site tells where to stay, what to see, and what to do in the BVI. Boat charter companies are also listed.

Cayman Islands

Caribbean On-Line: Cayman Islands

http://www.caribbean-on-line.com/cy/cy.html

Diving and beaches are the main attractions here; the Cayman Wall offers what may be the most spectacular wall dive anywhere.

Cuba

Destination Cuba

http://www.lonelyplanet.com/dest/car/cub.htm

Lonely Planet describes one of the world's last Communist nations as "the Caribbean's largest and least commercialized island."

If You Go to Cuba, Here's How to Do It

http://www.latinolink.com/travel/travel97/0524thow.htm

Most Americans are prohibited from visiting Cuba, but here's how many do it without getting caught.

Curaçao

Curaçao

http://www.interknowledge.com/curacao/

Dutch architecture, orchids, countless beaches, and cheap shopping draw tourists to this island off the Venezuela coast.

Dominica

Dominica: The Basics

http://www.delphis.dm/basics.htm

Ecotourism, diving, and sportfishing are Dominica's stock in trade. Bring plenty of film to capture the mountains, birds, tropical foliage, and waterfalls.

Dominican Republic

Hispaniola.com

http://www.hispaniola.com

This unofficial Dominican Republic Travel Guide has a special section on Cabarete, a windsurfer's paradise on the north side of the island.

Jay's Tour of the Dominican Republic

http://members.aol.com/jayventura/rd/repdom.htm

Jay Ventura, a Dominican living in the United States, describes his country and offers a useful selection of Web links.

Grenada

Grenada

http://www.grenada.org

Ronald Reagan's troops invaded the largest of "The Spice Isles" in 1983. Today, American visitors are more likely to shoot photographs than people.

Haiti

Haiti

http://caribbeantravel.com/cgi-bin/gb_msg.pl?
msg=destination&destination_name=Haiti

Don't let tales of voodoo or Papa Doc frighten you off; Haiti is again welcoming tourists.

Jamaica

Jamaica!

http://www.jamaicatravel.com

Play golf, soak up the sun at a ritzy resort, or climb a 600-foot waterfall in a country that "in many ways is more like a continent than an island."

Jamaica Tourist

http://www.jamaicans.com/tourist/

"It's the travel agent's job to sell you a package to Jamaica; it's our job to tell you what to expect and how to see Jamaica the way it was meant to be seen."

Martinique

Martinique

http://www.martinique.org

"The ever radiant welcome of Martinique" is offered in English or French.

Montserrat

Montserrat

http://24.3.19.68/montserrat/touristboard/

The Soufrière Hills Volcano has been erupting since 1995, so check http://volcano.und.nodak.edu/vwdocs/current_volcs/montserrat/montserrat.html before making travel plans.

Puerto Rico

Welcome to Puerto Rico

http://welcome.topuertorico.org

The Commonwealth of Puerto Rico is a mountainous island with rain forests, deserts, beaches, and the historic capital of San Juan.

Soc.culture.puerto-rico: San Juan FAQ

http://www.cis.ohio-state.edu/text/faq/usenet/puerto-rico-FAQ/faq-doc-22.html

Plain-text Web pages don't get any uglier than this, but the FAQ is a good introduction to San Juan and includes many Web links.

Saba

Saba

http://www.turq.com/saba/

Dutch is the official language of Saba, a dormant volcano that rises steeply from the sea. A marine park, dedicated in 1987, has a four-person recompression chamber for divers who get into trouble.

St. Barthélemy

St. Barths Online

http://www.st-barths.com/homeeng.html

St. Barts, a.k.a. St. Barths or Saint Barthélemy, is a glitzy but gracious haven for the moneyed set in the French West Indies.

St. Eustatius

St. Eustatius

http://www.turq.com/statia/

Saint Eustatius, nicknamed "Statia," is an island in the Dutch Antilles with a turquoise sea, black-sand beaches, and the second oldest synagogue in the Western Hemisphere.

St. Kitts and Nevis

St. Kitts and Nevis

http://www.stkitts-nevis.com

No building can be taller than the surrounding palm trees on these two islands, which are dotted with restored British fortresses and plantation inns.

St. Lucia

St. Lucia

http://www.interknowledge.com/st-lucia/

The French and British traded ownership of St. Lucia 14 times, maybe because neither could resist the island's twin peaks, wild orchids, tropical birds, and rain forests.

St. Martin/St. Maarten

St. Martin

http://www.interknowledge.com/st-martin/

The French and Dutch have shared this island for nearly 350 years. Now it's your turn.

St. Vincent and the Grenadines

Visit St. Vincent and the Grenadines

http://vincy.com/svg/

Princess Margaret owns an estate in these dramatically beautiful islands, which offer everything from wild parrots to ancient petroglyphs in addition to the usual yacht harbors and beaches.

Trinidad and Tobago

Trinidad & Tobago

http://www.visittnt.com

Join the party crowd at Trinidad's Carnival, or sample the quieter pleasures of "cool, serene, and green" Tobago.

Turks and Caicos Islands

Turks & Caicos Islands

http://www.interknowledge.com/turks-caicos/

One of the world's longest coral reefs makes these islands popular with divers. From the 230 miles of white beaches, you can watch whales and dolphins cavort offshore.

U.S. Virgin Islands

U.S. Virgin Islands Guide

http://www.usvi.net/

The United States bought the Virgin Islands from Denmark in World War I, and the capital of Charlotte Amalie is named after a Danish queen.

St. Croix

http://ecani.com/vi/sc/stcroix.htm

The largest island in the U.S. Virgins bills itself as "the best-kept secret under the American flag."

St. John Destination Page

http://www.travelfacts.com/tfacts/htm/stj/stjdest.htm

St. Thomas Destination Page

http://www.travelfacts.com/tfacts/htm/stt/sttdest.htm

These two sites have commercial listings, sightseeing tips, and maps.

MEXICO AND CENTRAL AMERICA

Latin America Traveler's Links Page

http://www.goodnet.com/~crowdpub/linksnew.htm

Find Web sites for countries throughout Central and South America.

Mexico

Travel Mexico
http://mexico-travel.com
The Ministry of Tourism's official Web site is ugly but functional.

Traveler's Guide to Mexico
http://www.travelmexico.com.mx
Plan your trip with the on-line version of a best-selling guidebook.

Mexico for Visitors
http://gomexico.miningco.com
Another MiningCo.com site with libraries of annotated links and a new article every week or two.

Mexico Connect
http://www.mexconnect.com
Tourism is just one topic here; click check "Destinations" and "Culture" for travel help.

Acapulco Net
http://acapulco-travel.web.com.mx/ing.html
Hotel listings are this site's strength.

Information Pages on Baja California
http://math.ucr.edu/~ftm/bajaInfoPage.html
Ignore the interface, and you'll find useful information.

Mexico City Virtual Guide
http://www.mexicocity.com.mx/mexcity.html
Hotels, restaurants, and general advice are on tap here.

Info San Miguel
http://www.infosma.com
San Miguel de Allende was once a Spanish Colonial town; today, it's an art colony with many American residents.

The Mayan Riviera

http://www.mayan-riviera.com

This site covers Cancún, Cozumel, Isla Mujeres, and other resorts with varying degrees of success.

Mysteries of the Maya

http://www.mysteriousplaces.com/Chichen_Itza_Page.html

Tour Chichén Itzá in photos and text.

Vive Guadalajara

http://www.vivegdl.com.mx/vivegdli.htm

The capital of Jalisco State is Mexico's second largest city. It's popular with American tourists, retirees, and mariachi fans.

Belize

Belize by Naturalight

http://www.belizenet.com

Read the No. 1 tourist guide to Belize (formerly British Honduras), a diving and fishing paradise that has the world's second largest barrier reef.

Costa Rica

Costa Rica

http://www.tourism-costarica.com

Ecotourism brings many North Americans to Costa Rica, a 150-year-old democracy that some call "the Switzerland of the Americas."

Cocori: Complete Costa Rica

http://www.cocori.com

Articles, maps, and photos make Cocori essential reading for tourists and potential residents.

El Salvador

Destination El Salvador

http://www.lonelyplanet.com.au/dest/cam/els.htm

Lonely Planet warns that El Salvador isn't geared to the
independent traveler; rather, it's suited to those who want to help a
country rebuild itself.

Guatemala

Guatemala

http://www.guatemala.travel.com.gt

Mayan history and culture are Guatemala's stock in trade; beach
resorts and rain forests are other attractions.

Destination Guatemala

http://www.lonelyplanet.com/dest/cam/gua.htm

Lonely Planet offers general tourist information for Guatemala,
including a warning about crime.

Honduras

Honduras.com

http://www.honduras.com

Some come for Spanish Colonial history; others for diving,
uncrowded beaches, and cheap prices.

Destination Honduras

http://www.lonelyplanet.com/dest/cam/hon.htm

"Honduras was the original banana republic," says Lonely Planet.

Nicaragua

Tourist Guide of Nicaragua

http://www.nicaragua-online.com/nic_eng.htm

Iván Olivares divides his country into eight regional journeys.

Destination Nicaragua

http://www.lonelyplanet.com/dest/cam/nic.htm

Lonely Planet discusses Central America's largest country from a historical, political, and traveler's perspective.

Panama

Welcome to Panama

http://www.panamatours.com

Be patient—these pages load with the speed of a megaship creeping through the Panama Canal.

Destination Panama

http://www.lonelyplanet.com/dest/cam/pan.htm

As usual, Lonely Planet provides a succinct and well-written tourist overview.

The Panama Canal

http://www.pancanal.com

Panama's biggest source of income is a sight worth seeing, preferably from a deck chair.

SOUTH AMERICA

General Information

South America for Visitors

http://gosouthamerica.miningco.com

Bonne Hamre, who writes articles and selects links for this site, grew up in South America and has a degree in Latin American Affairs.

Argentina

Argentina

http://www.sectur.gov.ar/g/menu.htm

South America's most European country is a blend of Spanish, Italian, and homegrown culture.

Argentinae.com

http://argentinae.com/english/

Don't miss the photographic tour of Argentina's regions.

My Beloved Buenos Aires

http://www.wam.com.ar/tourism/g/reg6/reg6.htm

The tango's birthplace is a cosmopolitan city of 11 million people.

Bolivia

The World Travel Guide: Bolivia

http://www.wtgonline.com/data/bol/bol.asp

Indian culture is predominant in Bolivia, a country that offers everything from tropical lowlands to eerie mountain landscapes.

Destination Bolivia

http://www.lonelyplanet.com/dest/sam/bolivia.htm

Another Lonely Planet guide; it calls Bolivia "the Tibet of the Americas."

La Paz

http://home.t-online.de/home/dobras/

Bolivia's capital is the world's highest, with an elevation of 11,910 feet.

Brazil

Brazil

http://www.embratur.gov.br

Embratur (the Brazilian Tourist Board) produces this official site.

Brazilinfo

http://www.brazilinfo.com

Come here for the hotel guide, which has 1600-plus listings.

Brazil Incentive & Tourism

http://www.bitourism.com

Under "Cities," you'll find brief descriptions with links to regional maps.

Virtual Trip to Brazil

http://www.vivabrazil.com

This site is a hodgepodge of English, Portuguese, and French text, but it covers much of the country.

Rio with Love

http://www.riowithlove.com

A guide to Brazil's most famous city, from the heights of Sugar Loaf to Copacabana Beach.

Ipanema.com

http://ipanema.com

Plan a trip to the beach, or read the "Rio for Beginners" section.

Brasilia's Home Page

http://www.civila.com/brasilia/

Brazil's modern capital was carved out of the jungle in the 1950s. Check the photos before you book a trip.

Chile

Chile Travel

http://www.chile-travel.com

All the tourist basics here, from cheap accommodations to transportation tips.

Go Chile!

http://www.gochile.cl

This commercial site has an excellent hotel search engine, with photos and other details for each hotel.

CHIP Travel

http://www.chiptravel.cl

The Chilean Information Project covers outdoor travel, from the Atacama Desert to tip of Tierra del Fuego.

Destination Chile & Easter Island

http://www.lonelyplanet.com/dest/sam/chile.htm

Read the facts, check the map, view the slide show.

Valparaiso

http://www.chileweb.net/valparaiso/

Learn about Chile's main seaport in English or Spanish.

Easter Island

http://www.netaxs.com/~trance/rapanui.html

Although it's 2000 miles from South America, this island of stone monoliths has been part of Chile since 1888 (see Figure 6–7).

FIGURE 6–7

Easter Island.

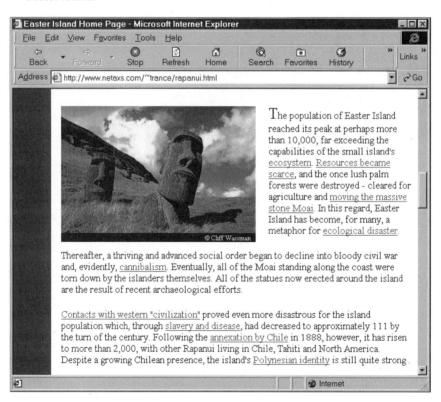

Colombia

Welcome to Colombia

http://www.colomsat.net.co/viajeschapinero/

This is a good introduction to the country, although it's short on practical tourist advice.

Colombia Turismo

http://www.uniandes.edu.co/Colombia/Turismo/turismo.html

If you can't read Spanish, paste the URL of each page into the AltaVista translation window at http://babelfish.altavista.com.

Destination Colombia

http://www.lonelyplanet.com/dest/sam/col.htm

Worried about cocaine cartels and guerrilla soldiers? Don't be, says Lonely Planet, which calls Colombia "the most underrated travel destination on the continent."

Guiaturismo de Colombia

http://www.guiaturismo.com.co

Also in Spanish, but the tourist listings make it worth the bother of translating with AltaVista.

Ecuador

Ecuador Explorer

http://ecuadorexplorer.com

This lively, readable site has regional information and detailed accommodations listings for continental Ecuador and the Galapagos Islands.

The FunkyFish Ecuador Guide

http://www.qni.com/~mj/

The name may be cute, but the information here is useful and down-to-earth.

Travelecuador

http://www.travelecuador.com/english/

Another good Ecuador site, with up-to-date news of weather and mountain conditions.

Via Ecuador

http://www.viaecuador.com

Regional and city information are this site's strengths.

Quito On-Line

http://www.quito.org

Ecuador's capital has enough museums, churches, and other landmarks to keep a culture buff occupied for weeks.

Guyana

Destination Guyana

http://www.lonelyplanet.com.au/dest/sam/guy.htm

Come for the waterfalls if you're adventurous, and don't dwell too long on Jonestown.

Paraguay

The Absolutely Unofficial Page of Paraguay

http://www.eskimo.com/~krautm/

The tourist content here is taken from Lonely Planet, but some of the other pages may be useful.

Destination Paraguay

http://www.lonelyplanet.com/dest/sam/par.htm

Lonely Planet calls Paraguay "a country little known even to its neighbors." Maybe it just needs an official Web site.

Peru

Trafico Online Peru

http://www.traficoperu.com/English/whoweare.htm

A hotel and restaurant database make this a vital stop on your planning itinerary; you'll also find transportation and sightseeing information.

Peru Explorer

http://www.peru-explorer.com

Learn about Peru's regions, ecotourism, and adventure travel.

Virtual Peru

http://www.xs4all.nl/~govertme/visitperu/

Descriptions and photos of Peru's regions, cities, and national parks make this site worth a visit.

Hike the Andes!

http://www.wp.com/andes/

Come in June, July, or August, and bring outdoor gear.

Lima

http://www.peruguide.com/ciudad/lima/lima.htm

This excellent site is in Spanish, but you can simply admire the photos if you don't want to translate the pages at http://babelfish.altavista.com.

Suriname

Destination Suriname

http://www.lonelyplanet.com.au/dest/sam/sur.htm

Suriname, formerly Dutch Guiana, is interesting mainly as a cultural melting pot with jungles.

Tropical Rainforest in Suriname

http://www.euronet.nl/users/mbleeker/suriname/suri-eng.html

Take a slideshow tour of the rain forest, using a nearby server for faster download times.

Uruguay

Uruguay

http://www.turismo.gub.uy/index-e.html

The Ministry of Tourism has menus in English, but many of the secondary pages are in Spanish.

Destination Uruguay

http://www.lonelyplanet.com.au/dest/sam/uru.htm

Lonely Planet describes tiny Uruguay as a "big-hearted" country with one of South America's most interesting capitals.

Venezuela

Venezuela in Postcards

http://www.postalven.com

Click the "English" link, then take a postcard tour of Venezuela's cities, towns, landscapes, and folklore.

Venezuela is Beautiful

http://venezuela.mit.edu/tourism/brochure/

This site portrays a nation that runs from the Caribbean coast to the Andes and the Amazon jungle.

Venezuela Tuya

http://www.venezuelatuya.com

"Venezuela Yours" has photos and regional descriptions. Scroll down for links to other resources.

Aqui se habla de Caracas

http://www.une.edu.ve/caracas/

Don't let the Spanish text keep you from enjoying this site on Caracas. You can translate the pages at http://www.babelfish.com.

Catholic Apparitions of Jesus and Mary

http://www.biddeford.com/~delorged/betania/

Travel one and one-half hours into the rain forest from Caracas, and you may witness a miracle.

Margarita Island

http://www.margaritaonline.com

Fly to the "Caribbean Pearl" from Caracas, or take a ferry from Puerto La Cruz or Cumaná.

EUROPE

Western Europe

General Information

Europe for Visitors

http://goeurope.miningco.com

My own European travel site has more than 100 illustrated articles on European travel topics and destinations, with 50-plus pages of annotated Web links (see Figure 6–8).

Andorra

Andorra

http://www.microstate.net/cgi-win/mstatead.exe/frame=http:/
www.xmission.com/~dderhak/andorra.htm

This tiny Catalan-speaking principality is in the heart of the Pyrénées, between France and Spain.

Austria

Austrian National Tourist Office

http://www.anto.com

The Austro-Hungarian Empire is gone, but Austria still provides a bridge between Alpine and Central Europe.

Innsbruck Tourism

http://www.innsbruck.tvb.co.at/ibk/innsbr-e.html

The Tyrol's capital is surrounded by ski areas.

Salzburg Information

http://www.salzburginfo.at

Mozart's birthplace is one of Europe's prettiest cities. (Tip: Book a hotel in the Old Town.)

Vienna Tourist Board

http://info.wien.at/e/

Come to the city of Strauss and *Strudel mit Schlag.*

FIGURE 6–8

Europe for Visitors.

The 1999 Carnevale di Venezia runs from Feb. 5-16.

Belgium

Belgian Tourist Office

http://www.visitbelgium.com

The world's best french fries are made in Belgium—and they're served with mayonnaise.

Hotels in Belgium

http://www.hotels-belgium.com

You won't find an easier-to-use hotel site than this one.

Brussels Capital Region

http://www.bruxelles.irisnet.be/en/homeen.htm

Follow the "Culture" and "Tourism" links to plan your trip.

Tourist Office for Flanders

http://193.75.143.1/toervl

Bruges, the best-known Flemish city, is the most popular tourist destination in Belgium.

Channel Islands

Guernsey Tourism

http://www.guernsey.net/~tourism/

Normandy is just a few miles from Guernsey and its neighboring islands of Alderney, Herm, and Sark.

Jersey Information

http://www.jersey.co.uk/jsyinfo/

Don't miss the German Underground Hospital, which was built by forced laborers from all over Europe in World War II.

Cyprus

Cyprus Tourist Page

http://www.kypros.org/Cyprus/tourist.html

Nicosia and other Greek enclaves occupy the larger part of this island in the Mediterranean.

North Cyprus

http://www.north-cyprus.com

The Turks claim the northern 37 percent of Cyprus, where Kyrenia is the most popular resort.

Denmark

Explore Denmark

http://www.geocities.com/TheTropics/4597/

For the world's best Danish pastries, go to the source. (And to get there, take a Scandinavian Seaways ferry from Harwich or Newcastle, England.)

Wonderful Copenhagen

http://www.woco.dk

Spend an evening at Tivoli, take a canal tour, and explore the capital's interesting museums.

Faroe Islands

Faroe Islands Travel Guide

http://www.puffin.fo/travel /

Smyril Line provides a weekly ferry service to this chain of rugged, scenic North Atlantic islands where people are outnumbered by sheep.

Finland

STN Travel Guide: Finland

http://www.stn.fi/english/

Finland's leading guidebook publisher serves up an exhaustive guide to Helsinki, North Lapland, and all points in between.

Helsinki

http://www.hel.fi/mato/

The Finnish capital celebrates its 450th anniversary in the year 2000.

France

France Tourism and Travel

http://www.fgtousa.org

The French Government Tourist Office in the United States has information on the home country and French territory from Tahiti to Martinique.

France for Visitors

http://gofrance.miningco.com

Doug Holaday provides hundreds of Web links and articles for travelers to France.

The Paris Pages

http://www.paris.org/parisfull.html

The French capital has many Web sites; this is unquestionably the best.

Paris Tourist Office

http://www.paris-touristoffice.com

If you're British, you'll have to grit your teeth as you click Old Glory for English text (see Figure 6–9).

FIGURE 6–9

Paris Tourist Office.

Côte d'Azur

http://www.crt-riviera.fr/crt-riviera/crt/uk_gp/gp_menu.html

Is it raining in Paris? Escape to the Riviera.

Germany

German National Tourist Office

http://www.germany-tourism.de

If you don't find everything you need here, try:

Germany for Visitors

http://gogermany.miningco.com

Explore 30-plus pages of annotated Web links and three years' worth of articles.

Lodging-Germany.com

http://www.lodging-germany.com/

Find hotel rooms quickly in 17 German cities.

Net4Berlin

http://www.net4berlin.com/home.e.html

With the Wall gone, Germany's reunified capital is booming.

City of Cologne Tourist Office

http://www.koeln.org/koelntourismus/english/

One and one-half million other people visit Cologne's Cathedral every year. Now it's your turn.

Frankfurt am Main Inform

http://www.frankfurt.de/index-e.html

If you're flying to Germany from North America, Frankfurt is likely to be your gateway.

Welcome to Munich

http://www.munich-tourist.de/english/offers.htm

Bavaria's largest city offers a lot more than Oktoberfest.

Gibraltar

Gibraltar Tourism

http://www.gibraltar.gi/tourism/home.html

See the Moorish Castle Complex, the Great Siege Tunnel, the 100-Ton Gun, and the Barbary Apes that roam the Rock.

Great Britain

British Tourist Authority

http://www.visitbritain.com

Plan a trip to England, Wales, Scotland, or Northern Ireland.

United Kingdom for Visitors

http://gouk.miningco.com

Jeff Clark, who lives in London, produces this comprehensive site.

Scottish Tourist Board

http://www.holiday.scotland.net

Beam yourself up with Scottish tourist, travel, and recreational advice.

LondonTown.com

http://www.londontown.com

The London Tourist Board serves up information and special offers for British and foreign tourists.

Edinburgh and Lothians Tourist Board

http://www.edinburgh.org

Stroll the Royal Mile, and attend the International Festival in August.

Greece

InfoXenios: GNTO

http://www.areianet.gr/infoxenios/english

Read the intro, then click the Greek National Tourism Organization link for help with trip planning.

Greece for Visitors

http://gogreece.miningco.com

Yet another MiningCo.com site, operated by a guide who leads tours of Greek ruins and wrote *The Mysteries of Isis.*

Athens Survival Guide

http://athensguide.com

Matt Barrett tells how to make the most of a visit to the city of Homer, the Gods, and ungodly traffic.

Iceland

Iceland Travel Net

http://www.arctic.is/itn/

Iceland is easy to reach by Icelandair; Smyril Line provides ferry service from Scandinavia and the Shetlands in summer.

Islandia

http://www.arctic.is/islandia/

Check the tourist info, then click "People" to find an Icelandic phrasebook.

Ireland

Ireland Tourist Board

http://www.ireland.travel.ie/home/

Check out more than 11,000 places to stay and 10,000 things to see and do.

Ireland for Visitors

http://goireland.miningco.com

Author Suzanne Barrett has expanded this site continuously since it made its debut in 1997.

Northern Ireland Tourist Board

http://www.ni-tourism.com

Tour Britain's outpost on the Emerald Isle.

Visit Dublin

http://www.visit.ie/dublin/

Pour yourself a Guinness and plan your trip to the city of Joyce, Shaw, Wilde, and Swift.

Isle of Man

Isle of Man

http://www.isle-of-man.com/

Manx Airlines or the Steam Packet Company will take you to this British Crown Dependency with a 1000-year-old parliament.

Italy

Italia

http://www.italiantourism.com

The Italian Government Travel Office (ENIT) has a new and modest Web site. For in-depth information, see:

Italian Tourist Web Guide

http://www.itwg.com

The tone here is unabashedly commercial, but you'll find everything you need from ferries to hotels.

Italy for Visitors

http://goitaly.miningco.com

Scott Holt writes articles and compiles annotated Web links to travel-related sites in Italy.

Your Way to Florence

http://www.arca.net/florence.htm

If you don't find what you need here, try Firenze.net at http://english.firenze.net.

Rome Guide

http://www.romeguide.it

Disregard the flashy graphics and spend a day or two digging through Rome's most comprehensive on-line guide.

Venice for Visitors

http://goeurope.miningco.com/mmore.htm

Personal plug: I manage this subsidiary site within Europe for Visitors, and it's the largest collection of Venice-related articles and links on the Web.

Liechtenstein

Principality of Liechtenstein

http://www.searchlink.li/tourist/

Switzerland's pint-size neighbor is just 4 miles wide by 16 miles long.

Luxembourg

Grand Duchy of Luxembourg

http://www.ont.lu

The National Tourist Office's home site isn't bad, but also see:

Luxembourg Tourist Office (London)

http://www.luxembourg.co.uk

This branch operation's pages should make the bosses in Luxembourg envious.

Malta

Malta at Your Fingertips

http://www.tte.ch/Malta/

Malta and neighboring Gozo are in the Mediterranean, 60 miles from Sicily, with 300 days of sunshine a year.

Monaco

Monaco

http://www.monaco.mc/usa/

Tour the Prince's Palace, see the Oceanographic Museum, and break the bank at Monte Carlo.

Netherlands

The Official Holland Site

http://www.visitholland.com

Tiptoe through the tulips, explore historic cities, or bathe along the North Sea Coast.

HotelRes
http://www.hotelres.nl
Search for hotel rooms throughout the Netherlands.

The Internet Guide to Amsterdam
http://www.cwi.nl/~steven/amsterdam.html
Steven Pemberton and Astrid Kerssens have put together a straightforward site with concise writing and useful links.

Tourist Board North-Holland
http://www.noord-holland-tourist.nl
Haarlem, the Hague, and Alkmaar are three of the cities featured here.

Welcome to Delft
http://www.dsdelft.nl/tourism/
The East India Company was headquartered in Delft during the seventeenth century; today, the city's major draws are historic atmosphere and fine porcelain.

Norway

Visiting Norway
http://www.norway.org
Scandinavia's most rugged nation is about the size of California, with uncrowded beaches and lovely fjords.

Virtual Oslo with a Guide
http://www.hurra.no/html/virtual_sightseeing.html
The English-language *Norway Post* sponsors this site.

Bergen for the Un-Tourist
http://home.sol.no/~vals/untourist.html
Even if you never get to Bergen, you'll enjoy reading Val Secretan's lively site.

Trondheim.com
http://www.trondheim.com/english/travel/
Norway's most noble city may be Trondheim, which has been a center of religion, scholarship, and trade for 10 centuries.

Portugal

Portugal

http://www.portugal.org/tourism

Scenic Portugal remains one of Europe's great bargains, and no country is friendlier to children.

Lisbon

http://www.eunet.pt/Lisboa/i/lisboa.html

Iberia's greatest coastal city could be described as "a San Francisco with sunshine and soul."

Virtual Portugal

http://www.portugalvirtual.pt/_tourism/

This site is organized geographically, with an emphasis on the Lisbon and Porto regions.

Algarve Tourist Board

http://www.rtalgarve.pt/inglish.html

Click the "Algarve" link for photos and fluff, or the information symbol for a list of tourist offices.

Dave's Alternative Guide to the Algarve

http://ourworld.compuserve.com/homepages/david_lynch/

David Lynch's pages are refreshingly noncommercial, if short on hotel and restaurant information.

San Marino

San Marino

http://inthenet.sm/rsm/intro.htm

It may be surrounded by Italy, but this tiny republic has been independent for almost 1700 years.

Spain

Spain

http://www.okspain.org

Three national cultures—Spanish, Catalan, and Basque—share a peninsula of green mountains, dry plateaus, and sunny islands.

All About Spain

http://www.red2000.com/spain/

Tour Spain by region, city, or letter of the alphabet.

Andalucía

http://www.andalucia.org/ing/homepage.html

Spain's sunny south is home to Córdoba, Granada, Jerez, Málaga, and Seville.

MadridMan's Yankee Home Page

http://www.madridman.com

He may live in Columbus, Ohio, but MadridMan is in love with the Castilian capital—and it shows in his pages.

Barcelona Online

http://www.barcelona-on-line.es/Angles/

Ignore the clumsy layout and get the information you need on Catalunya's capital.

Sweden

Sweden

http://www.gosweden.org

What do Greta Garbo, Ingmar Bergman, Alfred Nobel, Pippi Longstocking, and Abba have in common? They're all Swedes.

Sweden in Brief: CityGuide Sweden

http://cityguide.se/inbrief/

This site is updated frequently, so don't visit just once.

Stockholm

http://www.stoinfo.se/england/

The capital's official tourism site is plain but functional, like Swedish furniture.

Göteborg

http://goteborg.cityguide.se

Gothenburg is Sweden's second largest city, with excursion boats and amusement parks to tempt the summer tourist.

Malmö

http://www.malmo.se/eng/
In 2000, the Øresund Fixed Link bridge and tunnel will make today's ferries to Copenhagen obsolete.

Switzerland

Switzerland

http://www.switzerlandtourism.com
Buy a Swiss Pass, then tour Europe's most dramatic landscape by train, bus, boat, funicular, and cablecar.

Switzerland & Austria for Visitors

http://goswitzerland.miningco.com
Plan your Swiss or Austrian trip with Cheryl Imboden, my travel companion of 31 years.

Bern

http://www.berntourismus.ch
Visit Parliament, feed the bears, and shop beneath the arcades of the medieval city center.

Geneva

http://www.geneve-tourisme.ch
From Switzerland's United Nations city, take a lake steamer to Lausanne or Montreux.

Lucerne

http://www.luzern.org/index_e.html
Tourists flock here for the Lake of the Four Forest Cantons, the Swiss Transportation Museum, and two historic footbridges.

Zürich News

http://www.zuerich.ch
The banking capital of Switzerland is a delightful lakeside city where you can eat lunch or dinner on a "Gastrotram."

Vatican

The Holy See

http://www.vatican.va

If you don't find what you need here, try
http://www.christusrex.org.

Eastern Europe

General Information

Eastern Europe for Visitors

http://goeasteurope.miningco.com

Bill Biega supplies articles and Web libraries for 19 Eastern
European countries, from Albania to Yugoslavia.

Bulgaria

Bulgaria

http://www.travel-bulgaria.com

Folklore, ancient monuments and monasteries, and the Black Sea
Riviera make Bulgaria an intriguing change of pace for Western
tourists.

Croatia

Croatian National Tourist Board

http://www.htz.hr

If this site isn't working (as is sometimes the case), try the phone
and fax numbers at http://croatia.cronet.com/travel.html.

Czech Republic

Czech Republic—General Information

http://www.tourist-offices.org.uk/Czech_Republic/info.html

The info here is skimpy, but it's a start.

Czech Republic FAQ

http://www.fas.harvard.edu/~sever/Czech.homepage.html

Internet users have contributed heavily to this "frequently asked
questions" document, which includes a large section on Prague.

Hotels & Travel in the Czech Republic

http://www.hotelstravel.com/czech.html

Scroll down past the hotels for information on cities and towns.

Prague from A to Z

http://www.a-zprague.cz

The Prague City Server covers the capital and a growing number of other cities in the Czech Republic.

Prague I Guide

http://www.pragueiguide.com/guide/home.html

Listings of hotels, restaurants, cafés, and more, make this site worth a visit.

Prague Info Pages at SunSITE Czech Republic

http://sunsite.mff.cuni.cz/prague/

Click "Sightseeing" and "Culture" for detailed descriptions and useful links.

Hungary

Destination Hungary

http://www.lonelyplanet.com/dest/eur/hun.htm

Lonely Planet produces this unofficial site.

Hotels & Travel in Hungary

http://www.hotelstravel.com/hungary.html

Where to stay, with links to maps and a site for Budapest.

Globewalker's Guide to Budapest

http://www.globewalker.com

Start by reading the nine pages of essential facts, then find a hotel, and check sightseeing and other listings.

Latvia

Riga in Your Pocket

http://www.inyourpocket.com/rihome.htm

This on-line version of a first-rate travel guide covers Riga and other Latvian cities.

Lithuania

Vilnius in Your Pocket

http://www.inyourpocket.com/vihome.htm

The Pocket Guides team offer another outstanding book on a Baltic capital.

Poland

Poland

http://www.polandtour.org

In addition to general info, The Polish National Tourist Office has profiles of 13 cities.

Sport, Tourism, and Recreation

http://poland.pl/tourism/

The Official Web Site of Poland has extensive links to tourist information from various sources.

Welcome to Warsaw

http://owhc-ceer.fph.hu/pages/Cities/Warsaw/homepage.htm

A World Heritage Cities conference inspired this historical and photographic overview.

Krakow

http://www.krakow.pl/WK/EN/

Poland's capital from the eleventh to the seventeenth centuries is one of only 12 cities on the UNESCO World Heritage List.

Romania

Romanian Travel Guide

http://www.rotravel.com

Romanian Web links are often iffy, so visit http://home.sol.no/~romemb/tourism.htm if you get a server error.

Bucaresti

http://www.rotravel.com/counties/bucurest/

This Bucharest tourism site has sightseeing information, hotel listings, and a page for Romania's first youth hostel.

Russia

Russia

http://www.interknowledge.com/russia/

The "New Russia" is covered in text and photographs, with addresses and phone numbers for tourist offices in 15 countries.

Russia for Visitors

http://gorussia.miningco.com

Andrey Sebrant, a native Muscovite, serves up articles, Web links, and a Webcam from his Moscow apartment.

Moscow Guide

http://www.moscow-guide.ru

The Moscow government's tourism site is geared toward foreign visitors with fat wallets.

St. Petersburg Guide

http://www.guide.spb.ru

Cold War veterans will remember St. Petersburg as Leningrad, but it was a Czarist capital long before that.

St. Petersburg at Your Fingertips

http://www.cityvision2000.com

This site is especially useful for hotel listings and other commercial information.

Slovakia

Slovakia.org

http://www.slovakia.org/tourism/

Czechoslovakia's trisyllabic portion is now a country (and tourist destination) in its own right.

Ukraine

Paperless Guide to Ukraine

http://pages.prodigy.net/euroscope/guidetoc.html

This site has a nasty habit of changing URLs, so check my country links at http://goeurope.miningco.com if you can't find the home page.

Kyiv City Guide

http://www.uazone.net/Kiev.html

Kyiv, or Kiev, capital of the Ukraine, was featured in a 1997 movie, *A Friend of the Deceased.*

AFRICA

General Information

Africa for Visitors

http://goafrica.miningco.com

This may be your best starting point for articles and Web links on African travel.

Tourism in Africa

http://www.newafrica.com/tourism.htm

Newafrica.com offers detailed pages of tourist information for 18 African countries.

Ghana

Ghana

http://www.interknowledge.com/ghana/

For North Americans, Ghana (formerly the Gold Coast) has historic importance as a major center of the slave trade.

Kenya

Bwana Zulia's Kenya Travel Guide

http://www.bwanazulia.com/kenya/

This excellent site is enhanced by user contributions, including message boards and Melinda Atwood's *Jambo Mama.*

Morocco

Kingdom of Morocco

http://www.kingdomofmorocco.com

Royal Air Maroc introduces a fascinating North African country where I lived (and traveled) as a boy.

Morocco Bound

http://tayara.com/club/mrocbd1.htm

This site is directed at the independent traveler. It includes links to other Web sites.

Senegal

Senegal Online

http://www.senegal-online.com

More than 8 million African slaves were shipped from Senegal to North America and the Caribbean. Today, their descendants and other tourists come to relive history and see wildlife in national parks.

Republic of Senegal

http://www.earth2000.com/senegal/

The country's official homepage has tourist and historical information, including a page on the restored Gorée slave depot near Dakar.

South Africa

South Africa

http://www.satour.org

The South African Tourist Board describes "a world in one country" (see Figure 6–10).

South Africa Travel & Tourism

http://www.southafrica.net/tourism/

The South African embassy in Washington, D.C. produced this guide to the country and its regions.

Digital Guide to Tourism in Southern Africa

http://www.tourism.co.za

Whale watching, aviation tours, hiking itineraries, and places of interest are a few of the topics covered here.

FIGURE 6–10

South Africa.

Cape Town and the Western Cape

http://www.cape-town.net

Order a free visitors' guide or plan your trip with the links on the site.

Durban

http://www.durban.org.za/tourism/

Africa's busiest port has great beaches, Victorian landmarks, and historical museums. (For more on the latter, see http://armadillo.co.za/TimeTraveller.)

Pretoria

http://www.azania.co.za/south_africa/gauteng/pretoria

The capital of South Africa is in Gauteng Province, 40 miles from Johannesburg.

Tanzania

Tanzania Tourist Board

http://www.tanzania-web.com/home2.htm

"Africa's friendliest country" tempts adventure travelers with Mount Kilimanjaro, Serengeti National Park, dhow trips, and diving in the Indian Ocean.

Zanzibar Travel Network

http://www.zanzibar.net

Visit the historic Stone Town, tour spice plantations, or enjoy the island's more than 25 uncrowded beaches.

Tunisia

Tunisia

http://www.tourismtunisia.com

The Mediterranean country has long been popular with Northern Europeans for its seaside resorts, but a land of ancient Arab, Berber, Roman, and Phoenician sites is just a few miles inland.

Uganda

Tourism in Uganda

http://www.africa-insites.com/uganda/

The Nile River's source is in Uganda, and the country has 10 national parks. However, check the political situation before you come.

Zambia

Zambia

http://www.africa-insites.com/zambia/travel/

Victoria Falls is Zambia's "must-see" attraction. Other sights include the Livingstone Memorial, the world's largest chimpanzee sanctuary, and many national parks.

Zimbabwe

GORP: Zimbabwe

http://www.gorp.com/gorp/location/africa/zimbabwe/zimbabwe
.htm

Zimbabwe (formerly Rhodesia) shares Victoria Falls with Zambia.
Zambezi National Park is nearby.

Affordable Africa: Zimbabwe

http://www.afrizim.com

Accommodations, safaris, and packaged tours are featured here.

MIDDLE EAST

General Information

ArabNet

http://www.arab.net

Pick a country, then select "Tour Guide" for visa requirements and
other travel advice.

Egypt

Tour Egypt

http://touregypt.net

The Egypt Ministry of Tourism serves up travel information,
history, and an "I love Egypt" graphic souvenir for your Web page.

Egypt's Tourist Net

http://www.idsc.gov.eg/tourism/

Listings for hotels, restaurants, transportation companies, museums,
and more are available here.

Cairo

http://pharos.bu.edu/Egypt/Cairo/

History makes this site special, but you'll also find practical
information by clicking "Visitor Guide."

Alexandria

http://pharos.bu.edu/Egypt/Alexandria/

Egypt's legendary port has historic sites, museums, and beaches. The World War II battlefield and military museum at Al-Alamein is 65 miles west of the city.

Iran

Iran Tourism

http://www.itto.org

If you're intrepid (or foolish) enough to visit Iran, don't bring an Israeli passport, racy literature, fashion magazines, or anything that might offend the local regime.

Israel

Israeli Ministry of Tourism

http://www.goisrael.com

Israel bills itself as "the official destination of the Millenium," so accept no substitutes.

InIsrael

http://www.inisrael.com

Find a hotel and check for special deals from resorts and tour packagers. This site also has sections on Jerusalem, Nazareth, Tel Aviv, and other cities.

Jordan

The Hashemite Kingdom of Jordan

http://meltingpot.fortunecity.com/oregon/639/

You won't find hotel or restaurant listings here, but you can explore Jordan's regions with text and photos.

Lebanon

Lebanon Ministry of Tourism

http://www.lebanon-tourism.gov.lb

Lebanon and its cosmopolitan capital of Beirut are making a come-back as tourist destinations, thanks in part to a wealth of historic sites.

Palestine

A View from Palestine

http://travel.to/palestine/

Hotel listings don't provide much info, but the "Palestine, a Tour Guide" page has practical tips and sightseeing advice.

Saudi Arabia

ArabNet: Saudi Arabia Tour Guide

http://www.arab.net/saudi/tour/saudi_tour.html

Read the visa information before making any travel plans, because non-Muslim pleasure travelers aren't welcome here.

Syria

Visit Syria

http://www.visit-syria.com/

Looking for a reason to visit Syria? Damascus, the capital, is the oldest inhabited city in the world.

Turkey

Focus on Turkey

http://focusmm.com.au/tanamenu.htm

Look up information on sightseeing, hotels, cuisine, and other essential topics.

Travel Turkey

http://www.travelturkey.com

Practical information is the main draw here. Do-it-yourself travelers are well served, and a "Tour operators" page has URLs for companies that offer planned travel in Turkey.

Istanbul City Guide

http://www.istanbulcityguide.com

This massive site has a little of everything—including addresses of fast-food outlets like McDonald's and Pizza Hut.

INDIAN OCEAN

Mauritius

Mauritius

http://www.mauritius.net

Travel 1125 miles east of Mombasa, Kenya, and you'll find a tropical island that blends Indian, Chinese, French, Creole, and English cultures.

Seychelles

Seychelles Super Site

http://www.sey.net

Diving, snorkeling, and fishing are popular in this archipelago of 115 islands that lies 1000 miles east of the African continent.

ASIA

General Information

AsiaTour

http://asiatour.com

Diethelm Travel supplies facts and photos for eight Asian countries.

Peter M. Geiser's Internet Travel Guide

http://www.datacomm.ch/pmgeiser/

The author delivers succinct, matter-of-fact advice on traveling in Cambodia, China, Laos, Myanmar, Tibet, Vietnam, Indonesia, and Singapore.

Asia Travel

http://asiatravel.com

Hotel reservations are this site's main business, but it does offer practical information for 17 countries in Asia and the Pacific Rim.

South Asia for Visitors
http://gosouthasia.miningco.com
Andy McCord's site at MiningCo.com deals primarily with countries on the Indian subcontinent.

Bangladesh

Tour Bangladesh
http://venus.gsu.edu:8008/~mir/bangla/
Mir S Islam, a Bangledeshi living in Atlanta, offers a text and photo tour of his native country.

Bhutan

Kingdom of Bhutan
http://www.kingdomofbhutan.com
Bhutan, a gentle kingdom tucked between Tibet and India, attracts visitors with Himalayan scenery and Buddhist festivals.

Cambodia

Discover the Hidden Kingdom
http://home.hkstar.com/~1281868/cambodia.htm
Photos, basic information, and listings are here; for more tips on seeing Angkor Wat and avoiding trouble in Phnom Penh, see http://www.datacomm.ch/pmgeiser/cambodia.

China

China (CNTA)
http://www.cnta.com
China's official tourism site has a database of attractions, hotels, restaurants, and so forth, plus illustrated articles on the country's major attractions.

Dragon Tour
http://www.welleslian.com/dragontour/
This handsome site is sponsored by the Chinese government's publishing house for tourism.

The Beijing Page

http://www.flashpaper.com/yz/beijing/

A no-nonsense interface makes for fast-loading pages of links to other Beijing resources.

BeijingNow

http://www.beijingnow.com

Hotel info is skimpy, but information on shopping and other services is excellent here.

Hong Kong: City of Life

http://www.hkta.org

The Hong Kong Tourist Association offers in-depth information on the former British colony.

The Shanghai Guide

http://www.shanghaiguide.com/main/

China's largest city is "a place where mobile phones and designer clothes have replaced the blue Mao suits of the past."

India

TourismIndia.com

http://www.toursminindia.com

The Indian Ministry of Tourism operates this relatively new but ambitious site.

India Tourist Office, New York

http://www.tourindia.com

Use the clickable map for descriptions of India's many regions.

India Travel & Tourism

http://www.travel-library.com/asia/india/

This library of links includes tourism sites and travelogs.

Virtual Bangalore

http://www.virtualbangalore.com

The gateway to Southern India advertises itself as "The Garden City," although its flower exports are now taking a back seat to high tech.

Calcutta

http://pages.cthome.net/india2/

This site includes general impressions and practical advice, including how to volunteer at the Mother Teresa Mission.

Delhi

http://209.68.56.142/main.htm

Most foreign tourists arrive in Delhi, India's capital.

Indonesia

Tourism Indonesia

http://www.tourismindonesia.com

Java, Sumatra, and Bali are just three of Indonesia's 17,000-plus islands.

Jakarta OnLine

http://www.jakarta.go.id

The Dutch East India Company ran its spice trade here for 350 years; today, many of its 9 million people live and work in high-rises.

Japan

Japan Travel Updates

http://www.jnto.go.jp

The Japan National Tourist Organization has maps, FAQs, hotel listings, and a directory with links to regional and local tourist offices around the country.

Japan for Visitors

http://gojapan.miningco.com

Shizuko Mishima hosts this site, which has annotated Web links and biweekly articles on Japanese travel.

Traveling Cheaply to and in Japan

http://www.math.yale.edu/users/ravim/travel.html

Ravi Montenegro's tips are based on a year and a half of living in Japan on a student's budget.

Kyoto

http://web.kyoto-inet.or.jp/org/hellokcb/

Kyoto was the capital of Japan for 1000 years, and it remains the nation's cultural and spiritual home.

Osaka

http://www.tourism.city.osaka.jp/en/

A historic castle and the site of Universal City Japan are two examples of this bustling city's diversity.

Planet Tokyo

http://www.pandemic.com/tokyo/

This lively guide is filled with useful advice, but your eyes may not like the yellow-on-black page design.

A Little Help for Non-Japanese People Visiting Tokyo

http://www.parkcity.ne.jp/~geodesic/HelpVisitTokyo/

Buying tickets for Japanese subways and trains is the main theme here, but the links are also helpful and the dog animation is cute.

Laos

Destination Laos

http://www.lonelyplanet.com/dest/sea/laos.htm

Lonely Planet reports that, after 15 years of isolation, Laos once again offers an "unparalleled glimpse of traditional South-East Asian life."

Macau

Macau Tourism

http://macau.tourism.gov.mo

Portuguese traders settled in this tiny peninsula on the Southeast China coast in the 1500s, and Portuguese is still one of the two official languages.

Malaysia

Tourism Malaysia

http://tourism.gov.my

To sample this nation of "many faces and races" at close range, try the tourist office's homestay program.

Kuala Lampur Online

http://www.mnet.com.my/klonline/

Like Malaysia, KL is a place of contrasts, with everything from British colonial landmarks and Chinese market stalls to skyscrapers.

Sarawak Tourist Board

http://www.sarawaktourism.com

The "hidden paradise of Borneo" has tropical rain forests, orangutans, and ethnic groups dating back to the Stone Age (see Figure 6–11).

Myanmar

Destination Myanmar

http://www.lonelyplanet.com/dest/sea/myan.htm

Before booking a flight to Myanmar (formerly Burma), ditch your Amnesty International membership card and see the film *Beyond Rangoon.*

Nepal

Travel-Nepal.com

http://www.travel-nepal.com

Ancient Buddhist traditions and mountain trekking are two good reasons to visit this country, where you can ride an elephant and see Mt. Everest.

Pakistan

Pakistan

http://www.tourism.gov.pk

The Islamic Republic of Pakistan is one of Asia's most interesting countries, but traveling can be risky for Westerners.

FIGURE 6–11

Sarawak Tourist Board.

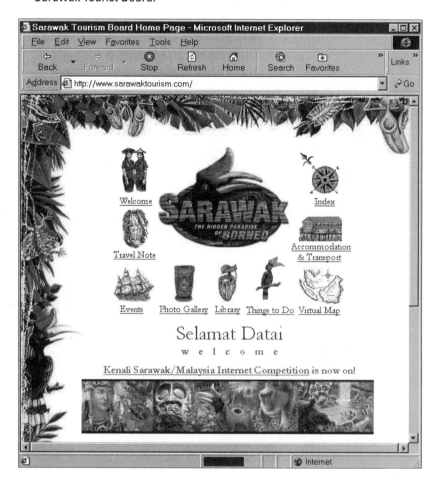

Destination Pakistan

http://www.lonelyplanet.com/dest/ind/pak.htm

Lonely Planet gives the pros and cons of a trip to Pakistan.

Karachi: The Quaid's City

http://www.alephx.org/karachi/

Pakistan's capital was a village 100 years ago; it's now a commercial center of 9 million people.

Philippines

The Philippines

http://www.tourism.gov.ph

More than 7000 islands make up this former Spanish and U.S.
colony. Must-see include Iatramuros, Corregidor, Baguio,
Pagsanjan Falls, and the rice terraces of Ifugao.

Destination Philippines

http://www.lonelyplanet.com/dest/sea/phil.htm

Lonely Planet calls Filipinos as "an exceptionally friendly and
helpful bunch," which jibes with my experience when I lived in the
Philippines as a boy.

Singapore

New Asia—Singapore

http://www.newasia-singapore.com

Tired of squinting at your monitor? Sit back and listen to the
RealAudio commentaries that are scattered throughout this site.

This Week Singapore

http://www.tws.com.sg/html/home.htm

Listings of sightseeing attractions, shops, restaurants, nightclubs,
and so on, are available here, but you may have to wait until next
week for the pages to download.

South Korea

Korea National Tourism Organization

http://www.knto.or.kr

South Korea is about half the size of England, with tourist
attractions that range from ancient temples to the world's most
heavily fortified border.

South Korea

http://web.mit.edu/royk/www/t-as-KO.html

This page is merely a list of links, but it'll point you to an array of
tourist information.

Seoul Focus

http://www.metro.seoul.kr/eng/

Click the "Travel" link or read other pages about South Korea's teeming capital of 10,300,000 people.

Sri Lanka

Ceylon Tourist Board

http://www.lanka.net/ctb/

Ethnic strife has made Sri Lanka less appealing than it once was. That may be the tourist board's reason for resurrecting the name "Ceylon," which evokes images of a less violent time.

Destination Sri Lanka

http://www.lonelyplanet.com/dest/ind/sri.htm

This honest description of the country and its problems includes a library of traveler's reports.

Taiwan

Tourism Bureau ROC

http://www.tbroc.gov.tw

Taiwan, once known as "Formosa," is a mountainous island of classical Chinese culture, aboriginal tribes, bamboo forests, and skyscrapers.

Visitor's Guide to Taiwan

http://peacock.tnjc.edu.tw/ADD/TOUR/main.html

This noncommercial site has good information and links to other resources.

Taipei Travel Guide

http://travel.cybertaiwan.com/taipei/

The Republic of China's capital has changed dramatically since I dodged oxcarts and rode pedicabs as a high-school student 35 years ago.

Thailand

Thailand

http://www.tourismthailand.org

Buddhist temples, ancient ruins, beaches, and memories of *The King and I* draw tourists to the Kingdom of Thailand.

Thailand Online

http://www.thailine.com/thailand/english/english.htm

This site's interface is a mess, but don't let that keep you from browsing.

Thailand Hotels & Tour Information

http://www.tiscoverasia.com/bangkokent/

Find accommodations in Bangkok and 17 other regions.

Bangkok: The Expat's Guide

http://www.geocities.com/Tokyo/Garden/1402/

You don't have to live in Bangkok to take advantage of Matt Pearson's sightseeing, restaurant, shopping, and other tips.

Vietnam

Vietnam Tourism

http://www.vietnamtourism.com

Nearly 25 years after the U.S. military's departure, the Socialist Republic of Vietnam has become a mecca for budget tourists with a taste for ancient culture and modern history.

Destination Vietnam

http://www.lonelyplanet.com/dest/sea/vietnam.htm

Lonely Planet offers background, practical advice, and traveler's reports for Vietnam-bound tourists.

Returns to Vietnam

http://grunt.space.swri.edu/visit.htm

Vietnam veterans and war buffs will find this site interesting; it offers trip reports, photos, maps, and even a language primer.

SOUTH PACIFIC/OCEANIA

General Information

South Pacific Islands Travel Channel

http://www.tcsp.com

American Samoa, the Cook Islands, Fiji, French Polynesia, and nine other destinations are featured here.

The South Pacific

http://www.hideawayholidays.com.au

Click this commercial site's "Destinations" links for pages on 13 Pacific islands and archipelagos.

Australia

Australian National Tourist Commission

http://www.aussie.net.au

You could spend days trolling this site. If you don't find the info you need, an "Aussie Helpline Travel Counsellor" will answer your questions by e-mail.

Australia for Visitors

http://goaustralia.miningco.com

Larry Rivera, a journalist and editor in Sydney, serves up Australian travel features and Web links.

Office of National Tourism

http://www.tourism.gov.au/TravelTips/

This "travel tips" page has links to state or territorial tourism agencies and Australian diplomatic missions worldwide.

Tourism New South Wales

http://www.tourism.nsw.gov.au

Your plane is likely to arrive in Sydney, so you'll be starting your Australian vacation here.

Cook Islands

Cook Islands

http://www.cook-islands.com

Rarotonga and Aitutaki are just two reasons to visit the Cook Islands, a Polynesian paradise that you can reach via Air New Zealand from Auckland or Los Angeles.

Fiji Islands

Fiji Islands

http://www.bulafiji.com

Come to Fiji's 330 islands for diving, surfing, visits to traditional Polynesian villages, and hikes through rain forests without poisonous snakes or spiders.

Rob Kay's Fiji Islands Travel Guide

http://www.fijiguide.com

Kay is the original author of Lonely Planet's Fiji guidebook, and he's covered the Fiji Islands as a journalist for 18 years.

Guam

Guam Visitors Bureau

http://www.visitguam.org

The largest island in the Marianas is a U.S. territory with six World War II historic parks. Its resorts attract nearly 800,000 Japanese tourists every year.

Marshall Islands

Republic of the Marshall Islands

http://www.hideawayholidays.com.au/trw_.htm

Diving and fishing are popular with visitors to the Marshalls, and there are many World War II shipwrecks around the islands.

Micronesia

Federated States of Micronesia

http://www.visit-fsm.org

Chuuk, Kosrae, Pohnpai, and Yap offer glimpses of traditional Micronesian culture in a widely scattered island chain just above the Equator (see Figure 6–12).

FIGURE 6–12

Federated States of Micronesia.

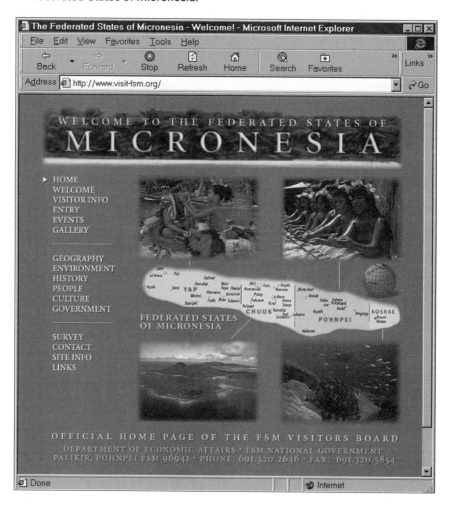

Destination Micronesia

http://www.destmic.com

This commercial site has information on FSM member states and other Micronesian islands, such as Guam, Palau, and the Marshalls.

New Caledonia

New Caledonia

http://www.noumea.com

Tribal accommodations offer a taste of local life in this French outpost 1100 miles east of Australia.

New Zealand

Passport to New Zealand

http://www.nztb.govt.nz

The New Zealand Tourist Board serves up the usual tourist information, plus links to other useful sites.

AA New Zealand Travel Guide

http://www.aaguides.co.nz

The New Zealand Automobile Association provides listings of sights, accommodations, and activities in 19 tourist regions.

New Zealand Travel Guide

http://www.travelenvoy.com/newzealand.htm

This site is heavy on commercial listings, but it's also jam-packed with local events and attractions.

Papua New Guinea

Tourist Promotion Authority

http://www.dg.com.pg/paradiselive/

All isn't paradise in PNG; for a more balanced picture, see:

Destination Papua New Guinea

http://www.lonelyplanet.com.au/dest/aust/png.htm

Lonely Planet discusses reasons to visit (or skip) a nation of wild landscapes, 750 languages, and limited infrastructure for travelers.

Tahiti

Tahiti Explorer

http://www.tahiti-explorer.com

The French Polynesian island of Tahiti is south of the Equator from Hawaii, just 7½ hours from Los Angeles by air.

Tonga

Kingdom of Tonga

http://www.vacations.tvb.gov.to

Tonga, in Western Polynesia, is popular with sailors of oceangoing yachts and whale watchers.

INDEX

TravelSeeker: Car Agencies, 34
TravelWeb, 54
TravLTips Freighter Cruise & Travel, 48
Trinidad and Tobago, 120
The Trip.com Flight Tracker, 28
Tunisia, 153
Turkey, 156–157
Turks and Caicos Islands, 120

Uganda, 153
U.K. Passport Agency, 15
Ukraine, 149–150
United Motorcoach Association, 31
United States:
   bus travel information, 31
   car rental services, 34
   destinations, 71–106
   rail travel information, 39–40
   states, 72–106
URL (Uniform Resource Locators), 2–3
Uruguay, 130–131
Usenet newsgroups, 24–25
U.S. Passport Services, 15
U.S. State Department, travel warnings
   and consular information sheets from,
   18–19
U.S. Virgin Islands, 120

Vatican, 146
Venezuela, 131

VIA Rail Canada, 39
Vietnam, 166
Villas, 56–57
Visa/Plus ATM locator, 20
Visas, 14–16
Visiting Britain: Car Hire and Travel, 37
Volunteering, 70

Weather and climate information, 22–23
WebFlyer, 30
Web indexes, 4–6
Web pages, download times for, 3
Web Search, 7–8
Web sites, address changes, 3
Western European destinations, 132–146
World Atlas and World Maps, 14
World Climate Weather, 23
Worldwide Brochures, 13
World Wide nest, 57
World Wide Sail, 51

Yachts, 50–51
Yahoo!, 4
   rentals information, 57
Youth hostels, 58–59
Yukon destinations, 113–114

Zambia, 153
Zimbabwe, 154

ABOUT THE AUTHOR

Durant Imboden is a travel writer and novelist who has visited or lived in more than 20 countries in the Americas, Europe, Africa, and Asia. He has worked in the travel industry and produces the *Europe for Visitors* Web site at http://goeurope.about.com.

CommerceNet is the premier organization for promoting and building electronic commerce solutions on the Internet. Visit their Web site at http://www.commerce.net.